SAY IT AS IT IS!

Learn to
SPEAK HAWAIIAN
Plus! Island Pidgin and Hanai Words
Authentic Easy Pronunciations

written by
MeneHune

illustrations by
Masaru Yamauchi

pronunciations by
Velda Yamanaka

edited by
Valjeanne Budar

Hawaiian Isles Publishing Co., Ltd.

Honolulu, Hawaii

Copyrighted in Japan, 1978, by Kyoiku Shuppan Co., Ltd. All Rights Reserved.
First edition printed in Japan, 1978. Second edition printed in U.S.A., 1982.

Inside front & back covers: Replicas of authentic Hawaiian petroglyphs discovered at various sites throughout the Islands. Petroglyphs, the Hawaiians' first form of communication, serve as an irreplaceable record of an aspect of ancient Hawaii that has, through analysis, provided a valuable insight into the culture and customs and traditions of the Polynesians' way of life long ago. There were three subject categories in Hawaiian petroglyphs; the descriptive, the symbolic and the cryptic. Petroglyphs were carved, pecked, chipped and scratched with stone hammers, pointed rocks or sharp pieces of basalt or other instruments upon such foundations as boulders, cliffs and lava rock. Through petroglyphs, the ancient Hawaiians would "Say It As It Is!"

Hanai (ha-NEYE) — Adopt.

INDEX

HERE IS YOUR EASY GUIDE
TO SPEAKING HAWAIIAN . . .
LIKE A HAWAIIAN!

I . . . pronounced *"i"*, is the shortest name in the Hawaiian language. It means: "The supreme one".

Then, from one extreme to another, one of the longest names is "Kekoalauli'ionapalihauliuliokeko'olau David Ka'apuawaokamehameha".

The name of one of Hawaii's tiniest fish, the "Humuhumunukunukuapua'a" is pronounced *HOO-mu-HOO-mu-NOO-ku-NOO-ku-AH-pu-WAH-'a.*

The Hawaiian language is considered by linguists to be one of the most fluid and melodious languages of the world. Only 12 letters appear in the Hawaiian alphabet. There are 5 vowels: *A, E, I, O, U.* And, there are only 7 consonants: *H, K, L, M, N, P* and *W.*

Every word in the Hawaiian language ends with a vowel and a vowel always appears between consonants; some words contain no consonants at all.

CONSONANTS

Sounds of consonants in Hawaiian closely resemble the sounds of English consonants, with one exception, the *W.* The letter *W* is pronounced in English when it follows *O* or *U* and as a soft *V* when it follows *E* or *I.* When *W* follows *A* or is the first letter in the word — the choice is yours to make.

VOWELS

Vowels in Hawaiian are pure vowels. In Hawaiian there are 2 sounds in each vowel, one of long, and the other of short duration. An example of this is the difference between the words *"pull"* and *"pool".*

SHORT VOWEL SOUNDS

(Indicated in lower case letters)

KAULELE*

a is like *"a"* as in *above*
e is like *"e"* as in *let, bet, bed*
i is like *"i"* as in *bit, tip, city, charity*
o is like *"o"* as in *so, open*
u is like *"u"* as in *pull*

LONG VOWEL SOUNDS

(Indicated in upper case letters)

A is like *"AH"* as in *father, palm*
E is like *"EH"* as in *eight, neigh, play, fete*
I is like *"EE"* as in *see, need, feet, police*
O is like *"OH"* as in *bone, sole, old, rose*
U is like *"OO"* as in *pool, room, rule*

INDIVIDUAL SYLLABLES

(Indicated by a DASH —)

Aloha, for example: *a-LOH-ha.*

SOUNDS OF HAWAII

GLOTTAL STOPS

(Indicated by a single quotation)

Some linguists consider the glottal stop as a true consonant. It is actually a minute pause or break in the air stream. If a glottal stop is not indicated between two vowels, the vowels are slurred together. In English, the glottal stop is the sound you hear between the o's when you say *"oh-oh"*.

DOUBLE VOWEL SOUNDS

Vowel combinations generally coalesce as a diphthong when the second is light or unaccented. Pronunciation for two adjoining vowels are commonly spoken as follows:

Ae and *Ai* are like *"i"* in *"eye"*, *"high"*, and *"line"*, but closing to short *"e"* and short *"i"*, respectively.
Ao and *Au* are like *"ow"* in *"how"* and *"cow"*, but closing to short *"o"* and short *"u"*, respectively.
Ea is like *"ea"* in *"pear"*.
Ei is like *"ai"* in *"raiment"*, *"wait"*, or *"a"* as in *"lay"*.
Ia is like the *"ier"* in *"pier"*; the initial *"i"* is pronounced like *"y"*, so for *"ia"* the sound is *"yah"*.
Iu is pronounced *"you"*; the initial *"i"* picking up the *"y"* sound.
Oa, is like *"a"* in *"all"* or *"awl"*.
Oe and *Oi* like *"oil"* or *"coy"* or *"boy"*, but closing to a short *"e"* and short *"i"*, respectively.
Ou is like the long *"o"*, closing to *"oo"*, as in *"zoo"*.

---

* KAULELE *(kow-LEH-le)* . . . to accent in music.

4

PEOPLE, PLACES, THINGS 'N TERMS IN HAWAIIAN

A'A *(AH-'AH)*
A rough broken kind of lava erupted from volcanoes.

A'ALA *(a-'AH-la)*
Fragrant.

AE *(EYE)*
Yes.

AHI *(AH-hi)*
Fire.

AHIAHI *(AH-hi-YAH-hi)*
Evening.

AI *(EYE)*
To eat.

AIKANE *(eye-KAH-ne)*
Friend.

AINA *(EYE-na)*
Land.

AKA'AKA *(AH-ka-'AH-ka)*
Laughter.

WAHINE MALIHINI

KEIKI MALIHINI

KEIKI MALIHINI

KANE MALIHINI

AKAMAI *(AH-ka-MEYE)*
Wise, smart, clever, expert.

AKUA *(a-KOO-wa)*
God, goddess, spirit, idol; more often called TIKI *(TEE-KEE)*, a Maori word.

ALA *(AH-la)*
Street.

ALANUI *(a-la-NOO-wi)*
Big road; highway or avenue.

ALII *(a-LEE-'i)*
Chief (s), king, royalty, highest nobility.

AKUA

HALE *(HAH-le)*
House; building.

HALE KEAKA *(HAH-le ke-AH-ka)*
Theater.

HALE KUAI *(HAH-le ku-WEYE)*
Store.

HALE KULA *(HAH-le KOO-la)*
School house.

HALE LEKA *(HAH-le LEH-ka)*
Post Office.

HALE MA'I *(HAH-le MAH-'i)*
Hospital.

ALOHA *(a-LOH-ha)*
Love, affection, welcome,
hello, good-bye.

ANU *(AH-nu)*
Cold.

AOLE *(a-OH-le)*
No.

AOLE PILIKIA *(a-OH-le pi-li-KEE-ya)*
No bother, no trouble.

AUWAI *(ow-WEYE)*
Brook.

AUWE *(ow-WAY)*
An exclamation; Oh!; Alas!

'AUMAKUA *('OW-ma-KOO-wa)*
Family or personal god.

ELE'ELE *(EH-le-'EH-le)*
Dark.

ELEMAKULE *(EH-le-ma-KOO-le)*
An old man.

HA'AKEI *(HAH-'a-KAY)*
Vain.

HAKU *(HAH-ku)*
Master.

HAKU MELE *(HAH-ku MEH-le)*
"To weave song"; hence, a poet.

HE'E

HALE MAKA'I *(HAH-le ma-KAH-'i)*
Police station.

HALE MOE *(HAH-le MOY)*
Hotel.

HALE PA'AHAO *(HAH-le pa-'a-HOW)*
Jail; prison.

HALEPOHAKU *(HAH-le-po-HAH-ku)*
Stone house.

HALEPULE *(HAH-le-POO-le)*
Church.

HANA *(HAH-na)*
Work; activity.

HANAI *(ha-NEYE)*
Adopt.

HANA PA'A *(HAH-na PAH-'a)*
Make fast.

HANAU *(ha-NOW)*
To be born.

HANOHANO *(HAH-no-HAH-no)*
Honorable.

HAOLE *(HOW-le)*
Caucasian; originally, any foreigner.

HAPA *(HAH-pa)*
A part; half.

HAPA HAOLE *(HAH-pa HOW-le)*
A person part Caucasian and part
another racial extraction.

HAPAI *(ha-PEYE)*
To lift; to carry; pregnant.

HAUOLI *(how-OH-li)*
Glad; happy; rejoice; joy.

HAWAII NEI *(ha-WEYE-'i NAY)*
"All our beautiful, beloved islands
of Hawaii".

HEENALU

WAHINE   KANE   iPO

HEʻENALU *(HEH-ʻe-NAH-lu)*
Surfing.

HEIAU *(HEH-i-YOW)*
Ancient temple, a pre-Christian place of worship.

HELE *(HEH-le)*
To walk; to go.

HELE MAI *(HEH-le MEYE)*
Come.

HIʻI *(HEE-ʻi)*
To hold in one's arms or embrace.

HIKI *(HEE-ki)*
To be able to do a thing; okay.

HIKIEʻE *(HEE-ki-AY)*
A broad bed; large Hawaiian couch.

HILAHILA *(HEE-la-HEE-la)*
Shy; bashful; ashamed.

HOʻE *(HOH-ʻe)*
Paddle.

HOKELE *(ho-KEH-le)*
Hotel.

HOLOHOLO *(HOH-lo-HOH-lo)*
To go traveling.

HOLOHOLONA *(HOH-lo-ho-LOH-na)*
Animal.

HONI *(HOH-ni)*
Kiss

HOʻOKANA *(HOH-ʻo-KAH-na)*
Proud.

HOʻOKANAKA *(HOH-ʻo-ka-NAH-ka)*
Brave.

HOʻOKUPU *(HOH-ʻo-KOO-pu)*
Gift.

HOʻOLAULEA *(HOH-ʻo-low-LEH-ya)*
A festival, happy event, picnic.

HOʻOMALIMALI *(HOH-ʻo-MAH-li-MAH-li)*
Flattery; to tease.

HOʻONUINUI *(HOH-ʻo-NOO-wi-NOO-wi)*
An exaggeration.

HUHU *(HOO-HOO)*
Angry; offended.

HUI *(HOO-i)*
An association; group, club·

HUKI *(HOO-ki)*
Pull.

HULI *(HOO-li)*
To turn; to curl over; to change,
as an opinion or manner of living.

IA *(EE-a)*
Fish or any marine animal, or eel,
oyster, crab, whale.

IHE *(EE-he)*
Spear.

IKAIKA *(i-KEYE-ka)*
Strong; powerful

IKE *(EE-ke)*
See; know.

IKI *(EE-ki)*
Small

IPO *(EE-po)*
Sweetheart; lover; darling.

KA'A *(KAH-'a)*
Car.

IHE

KAHILI *(ka-HEE-li)*
Feather standard, symbolic of royalty,
the original Hawaiian equivalent for a flag
or banner.

KAHUNA *(ka-HOO-na)*
An expert, a priest, minister,
or religious leader.

KALA *(KAH-LAH)*
Money.

KAMAAINA *(KAH-ma-EYE-na)*
Citizen of long standing, native-born
or old timer; a person born in Hawaii,
literally "child of the land".

KAMAILIO *(ka-MEYE-LEE-yo)*
To converse.

KANAKA *(ka-NAH-ka)*
Man; human being.

KANE *(KAH-ne)*
Male.

KAPAKAHI *(KAH-pa-KAH-hi)*
Crooked; one-sided.

KAPU *(KAH-pu)*
Prohibited; forbidden; keep out; tabu.

KAUKA *(KOW-ka)*
Doctor.

KAPU
DO NOT PICK FRUIT.

KUUIPO

KAULANA *(kow-LAH-na)*
Famous.

KAWAIAHAO *(ka-WEYE-ya-HAH-ʻo)*
Name of the foremost native church in
Honolulu, known as the Westminster
Abbey of Hawaii.

KEIKI *(KAY-ki)*
Child, children.

KILAKILA *(KEE-la-KEE-la)*
Majestic.

KINIPOPO *(KEE-ni-POH-POH)*
On the ball; right on.

KIPUKA *(ki-POO-ka)*
An opening.

KOA *(KOH-wa)*
Brave.

KOKUA *(ko-KOO-wa)*
Help; to cooperate; aid.

KOLOHE *(ko-LOH-he)*
Rascal, mischievous (good or bad).

KOMO *(KOH-mo)*
Enter.

KUAʻAINA *(KOO-wa-ʻEYE-na)*
Countryfield.

KULA *(KOO-la)*
School.

KULA KIʻEKIʻE *(KOO-la KEE-ʻe-KEE-ʻe)*
High School.

KULA NUI *(KOO-la NOO-wi)*
University.

KULEANA *(KOO-le-AH-na)*
Private property; responsibility;
jurisdiction; an ownership; homestead.

KULIKULI *(KOO-li-KOO-li)*
Be still.

KUMU *(KOO-mu)*
Teacher.

KUʻUIPO *(KOO-ʻu-EE-po)*
My sweetheart.

LAMALAMA *(LAH-ma-LAH-ma)*
Torch fishing.

LANAI *(la-NEYE)*
A porch; balcony; veranda; terrace.

LAPUWALE *(LAH-pu-WAH-le)*
Worthless.

LAULEʻA *(low-LEH-ʻa)*
Peace; friendship.

LAWA *(LAH-wa)*
Enough.

LEI *(LAY)*
Necklace; wreath; garland made with flowers, leaves, nuts or shells.

LEKA *(LEH-ka)*
Letter.

LELE *(LEH-le)*
Jump; leap; fly.

LIKE PU *(LEE-ke POO)*
The same.

LOA *(LOH-wa)*
Very long.

LOHI *(LOH-hi)*
Slow; late; tardy.

LO'IHI *(lo-'EE-hi)*
Tall; height.

LOLO *(LOH-LOH)*
Dumb.

LUA *(LOO-wa)*
Restroom.

LUAHINE *(LOO-wa-HEE-ne)*
Old woman.

LUAU *(LOO-'OW)*
Hawaiian feast.

LUHI *(LOO-hi)*
Fatigue.

LUNA *(LOO-na)*
Upper, foreman; overseer.

LUNA NUI *(LOO-na NOO-wi)*
Big Boss.

MA'ALAHI *(MAH-'a-LAH-hi)*
Easy; simple.

MAEMAE *(MAH-e-MAH-e)*
Clean.

MAHELE *(ma-HEH-le)*
Division.

MAHI'AI *(MAH-hi-'EYE)*
Farmer.

MAHOPE *(ma-HOH-pe)*
Later; bye and bye.

MAI *(MEYE)*
Sick.

MAIKA'I *(meye-KAH-'i)*
Good; fine; well; good-looking;
goodness; beautiful.

MAILE *(MEYE-le)*
Quiet; still; calm; a perfumed vine
used in garlands by Hawaii's royalty.

MAKAHIKI *(MAH-ka-HEE-ki)*
Year; also name given to ancient
Hawaiian harvest festival
celebrated annually.

MAKA'I *(ma-KAH-'i)*
Policeman.

MAKANA *(ma-KAH-na)*
Gift.

MAKAU *(ma-KOW)*
Afraid.

MAKEMAKE *(MAH-ke-MAH-ke)*
Wish; to desire.

MAKEPONO *(MAH-ke-POH-no)*
A good bargain; cheap.

MALALO *(ma-LAH-lo)*
Below.

MALIHINI *(ma-li-HEE-ni)*
A stranger; newcomer; visitor; tourist.

MALIMALI *(MAH-li-MAH-li)*
Flattery; to soothe; quiet.

MALUNA *(ma-LOO-na)*
Above.

MAMALU *(ma-MAH-lu)*
Umbrella.

MANA *(MAH-na)*
Power.

MANAPA'A *(MAH-na-PAH-'a)*
To fasten.

MANAWA *(ma-na-WAH)*
Time.

MANAWAHI *(ma-na-WAH-hi)*
Free; extra.

MAUNA *(MOW-na)*
Mountain.

MEA ALOHA *(MAY-ya a-LOH-ha)*
Beloved.

PILIKIA!

12

'OLI 'OLI

MEHA *(MAY-ha)*
Lonely.

MELE *(MEH-le)*
Song; chant.

MENEHUNE *(MEH-ne-HOO-ne)*
Legendary Hawaiian type of elf, said
to have worked at night and were
noted for doing good deeds.

MI'I *(MEE-'i)*
Attractive.

MIKI *(MEE-ki)*
Energetic; active.

MIKIOI *(MEE-ki-OY)*
Neat; nice.

MINOAKA *(MEE-no-AH-ka)*
To smile.

MOE *(MOY)*
To sleep.

MOI *(MOY)*
Sovereign; the King.

MOKU *(MOH-ku)*
Island.

MOMI *(MOH-mi)*
Pearl.

MOMONA *(mo-MOH-na)*
Fat.

NALU *(NAH-lu)*
Surf on the beach.

NANI *(NAH-ni)*
Pretty; beautiful.

NOHO *(NOH-ho)*
To sit; dwell.

NOU *(NOH)*
Yours.

NUI *(NOO-wi)*
Big; very.

OE *(OY)*
You.

'OLI'OLI *('OH-li-'OH-li)*
Much happiness.

'OLU'OLU *('OH-lu-'OH-lu)*
Congenial; friendly.

ONAONA *(o-NOW-na)*
Fragrance; perfume.

ONE *(OH-ne)*
Sand.

ONO *(OH-no)*
Sweetness; food to eat; tasty.

'OPIOPIO *('o-PEE-yo-PEE-yo)*
Young.

PAHU *(PAH-hu)*
Drum; barrel; box; keg.

MENEHUNE

13

PAKALAKI *(PAH-ka-LAH-ki)*
Unlucky.

PAKAUKAU *(pa-KOW-KOW)*
Table.

PAKIPIKA *(PAH-ki-PEE-ka)*
Pacific.

PALAPALA *(PAH-la-PAH-la)*
Writing.

PALI *(PAH-li)*
Cliff.

PANINI *(pa-NEE-ni)*
Cactus.

PANIOLO *(PAH-ni-OH-lo)*
Hawaiian cowboy.

PAPAHE'ENALU *(PAH-pa-HEH-'e-NAH-lu)*
Surfboard.

PAU *(POW)*
Finished; done; the end.

PA'U *(PAH-'u)*
Sarong.

PELE *(PEH-le)*
Goddess of Volcanoes.

PILAU *(pi-LOW)*
Bad smell; decayed; rotten.

PILIKIA *(PEE-li-KEE-ya)*
Trouble.

PIULA *(PYOO-la)*
Tired; exhausted.

POHAKU *(po-HAH-ku)*
Stones.

POHO *(POH-HOH)*
"Out of luck"; loss; damage.

POKO *(POH-KOH)*
Short.

POLOLEI *(POH-LOH-LAY)*
Straight; correct; fine.

POLOLI *(po-lo-LEE)*
Hungry.

POMAIKA'I *(po-meye-KAH-'i)*
Good luck; fortunate.

PONO *(POH-no)*
Right; lawful.

PUKA *(POO-ka)*
Hole; space; entrance.

PUKE *(POO-ke)*
Book.

PULU *(POO-lu)*
Wet.

PUNA *(POO-na)*
A spring.

PUNEE *(POO-ne-'e)*
Couch; settee; small bed.

PUPULE *(pu-POO-le)*
Crazy; daffy; looney; insane.

MEA PA'ANI

WA'A *(WAH-'a)*
Canoe.

WAHINE *(wa-HEE-ne)*
Female.

WAIWAI *(WEYE-WEYE)*
Rich.

WALA'AU *(wa-la-'OW)*
Talk; speak.

WELA *(WEH-la)*
Warm; hot.

WIKIWIKI *(WEE-ki-WEE-ki)*
Quickly; hurry; fast.

HAWAII'S CALABASH OF KAUKAU* TERMS

LUAU

'AHI *('AH-hi)*
Albacore or yellow tuna; a favorite for "sashimi", a Japanese term for "raw fish pupu".

'A'I *('AH-'i)*
Food.

'AINA *('EYE-na)*
Meal.

'AKU *('AH-ku)*
An ocean bonito.

ALANI *(a-LAH-ni)*
Orange.

'ELEKUMA *('e-le-KOO-ma)*
Small crabs.

HALA-KAHIKI *(HAH-la-ka-HEE-ki)*
Pineapple.

HALE 'AINA *(HAH-le 'EYE-na)*
Restaurant.

HAUPIA *(how-PEE-ya)*
A coconut cream pudding made from fresh coconut milk thickened with taro root. A luau dessert, it is cut into small squares.

HE'E *(HEH-'e)*
Squid; octopus.

HE'I *(HEH-'i)*
Good for digestion and as a meat tenderizer.

HIPA *(HEE-pa)*
Sheep.

HUA *(HOO-wa)*
Fruit.

HUAMOA *(HOO-wa-MOH-wa)*
Egg.

HUE *(HOO-we)*
Gourds used as containers to hold cooked foods.

HUKILAU *(HOO-ki-LOW)*
Ancient Hawaiian method of group fishing with a net, which is still popular today.

I'AIKI *(i-'EYE-ki)*
Rice.

I'A MAKA *(EE-'a MAH-ka)*
Raw fish.

I'A MALO'O *(EE-'a ma-LOH-'o)*
Dried fish.

*KAUKAU *(KOW-KOW)* — Pidgin for food.

I'A MIKOMIKO
(EE-'a MEE-ko-MEE-ko)
Salt fish.

IMU *(EE-moo)*
Earth oven.

INA MONA *(EE-na MOH-na)*
Kukui nut relish.

INU *(EE-nu)*
Drink.

I'O HIPA *(EE-'o HEE-pa)*
Mutton.

I'O PIPI *(EE-'o PEE-pi)*
Beef.

I'O PUA'A *(EE-'o pu-WAH-'a)*
Pork.

IPU HAOLE *(EE-pu HOW-le)*
Watermelon.

IPU PU *(EE-pu POO)*
Squash.

KALO *(KAH-lo)*
Taro, the treasured tuber of the
Islands. Sliced and deep fried, it
makes a dip or mashed with water
for poi. Leaves, cooked are
similar to spinach.

KALUA *(ka-LOO-wa)*
Method of cooking underground
in an imu (earth oven), such as
Kalua pig for luau; to bake.

KAPIKI *(ka-PEE-ki)*
Cabbage.

KAUKAU *(KOW-KOW)*
Pidgin expression for food.
(Not a Hawaiian word.)

KI *(KEE)*
Tea.

KO *(KOH)*
Sugar cane. Children enjoy
chewing it. It is frequently used
as a swizzle stick in Hawaiian
drinks such as a Mai Tai.

KO PA'A *(KOH PAH-'a)*
Sugar.

KOPE *(KOH-pe)*
Delicious beans grown on the Kona
Coast of the Big Island, the only
place in the United States where
coffee is grown.

KUKE *(KOO-ke)*
To cook.

16

HUKILAU

KUPA *(KOO-pa)*
Soup.

LAMA *(LAH-ma)*
Liquor; rum.

LAULAU *(LOW-LOW)*
Butterfish, pork, sweet potatoes or yams, and taro leaves steamed together in a pouch.

LILIKOI *(li-li-KOY)*
Passion fruit, usually served as a juice or sherbet.

MEA 'AI

LIMU *(LEE-mu)*
Seaweed, usually served as a salad item at a luau.

LOMILOMI *(LOH-mi-LOH-mi)*
To massage, rub, press, mash fine; also a masseur, masseuse.

LOMI SALMON *(LOH-mi)*
Massage-type preparation for readying salted salmon, shredded and mixed with tomatoes and onion.

LUAU *(LOO-'OW)*
Name for a Hawaiian feast.

MAIA *(ma-EE-ya)*
Banana.

MAI TAI *(MEYE-TEYE)*
Popular Polynesian drink.

MAKEKE *(ma-KEH-ke)*
Mustard.

MALAKEKE *(MAH-la-KEH-ke)*
Molasses.

MAUI ONION *(MOW-wi)*
A large, white, especially juicy and sweet onion grown on the Valley Island of Maui.

MEA 'AI *(MEH-ya 'EYE)*
Food.

MEA 'ONO *(MEH-ya 'OH-no)*
Cake.

MELI *(MEH-li)*
Honey.

MOA *(MOH-wa)*
Hawaiian word for fowl,
usually chicken.

NI'OI *(ni-'OY)*
Pepper.

NIU *(NEE-yu)*
Coconut.

OHIA *(o-HEE-ya)*
Mountain apple.

OKOLEHAO *(o-KOH-le HOW)*
Famous island liquor distilled from
the root of the ti plant.

OLEPE *(o-LEH-pe)*
Oysters.

OPIHI *(o-PEE-hi)*
Limpets from the sea. Served raw,
it is highly prized.

NIU

POI

PA'AKAI *(PAH-'a- KEYE)*
Hawaiian rock salt, often
dried from the sea. Some
salts are white, some red.

PAINA *(PEYE-na)*
Eat.

PALAOA *(pa-la-OH-wa)*
Flour.

PAPAI *(pa-PEYE)*
Crab.

PAPAPA *(pa-PAH-pa)*
Beans.

PELENA *(pe-LEH-na)*
Bread.

PIA *(PEE-ya)*
Beer.

PIPI KAULA *(PEE-pi KOW-la)*
Dried beef, often sirloin, salted and tastes like beef jerky.

PIPI 'OMA *(PEE-pi 'OH-ma)*
Roast beef.

PIPI PALAO *(PEE-pi pa-LOW)*
Beef steak.

POHA *(po-HAH)*
A rather hard to find, small wild orange-skinned berry. Makes a superb jam.

POI *(POY)*
A mashed tuber (taro root) which, like potatoes and rice are staple foods of Haoles and Orientals, poi is the staple food of Hawaiians.

PUA'A *(pu-WAH-'a)*
The king of a Hawaiian luau, a pig or hog.

PUPU *(POO-pu)*
Hors d'oeurve.

U'ALA KAHIKI *(u-AH-la ka-HEE-ki)*
Irish potato.

U'ALA MAOLI *(u-'AH-la ma-OH-li)*
Sweet potato.

'UHA PUA'A *('OO-ha pu-WAH-'a)*
Ham.

'UHI *('OO-hi)*
Yam.

WAI *(WEYE)*
Fresh water.

WAI MOMONA *(WEYE mo-MOH-na)*
Punch; soda.

WAIU *(WEYE-yu)*
Milk.

WAIUPAKAPAKA
(WEYE-yu-PAH-ka-PAH-ka)
Butter.

WAIUPAKAPA'A
(WEYE-yu-PAH-ka-PAH-'a)
Cheese.

19

SAY IT AS IT IS
HAWAIIAN STYLE!

DIRECTIONS

AKAU *(a-KOW)* . . . . North

HEMA *(HEH-ma)* . . . . South

HIKINA *(hi-KEE-na)* . . . . East

KOMOHANA *(KOH-mo-HAH-na)* . . . . , ... West

EWA *(EH-va)* . . . . Opposite Diamond Head

KAI *(KEYE)* . . . . Sea, ocean

KONA *(KOH-na)* . . . . Leeward, The South or Southwest;

KOOLAU *(KOH-'o-LOW)* . . . . Windward, North

MAKAI *(ma-KEYE)* . . . . Toward the sea.

MAUKA *(MOW-ka)* . . . . . . Toward the mountain

MOANA *(mo-WAH-na)* . . . . Ocean

KOKO HEAD *(KOH-ko)* . . Beyond Diamond Head.

PALI *(PAH-li)* . . . . Precipice or cliff.

UKA *(OO-ka)* . . . . In the mountains.

WAENA *(WEYE-na)* In between the mountains.

WAIMEA *(WEYE-MEH-ya)* . . . . Reddish
water; name applied to special localities.

HAWAIIAN TIME!

MAHINA *(ma-HEE-na)* . . . . Lunar month

MALAMA *(ma-LAH-ma)* . . . . Solar month

MAKAHIKI *(ma-ka-HEE-ki)* . . . . Year

KEKONA *(ke-KOH-na)* . . . . Second

MINUKE *(mi-NOO-ke)* . . . . Minute

HOLA *(HOH-la)* . . . . Hour

LA *(LAH)* . . . . Day

HEPEKOMA *(he-pe-KOH-ma)* . . . . Week

COUNT TO TEN

TRY IT IN HAWAIIAN!

EKAHI *('e-KAH-hi)* . . . . . . One

ELUA *('e-LOO-wa)* . . . . Two

EKOLU *('e-KOH-lu)* . . . . . . Three

EHA *('e-HAH)* . . . . Four

ELIMA *('e-LEE-ma)* . . . . . . Five

EONO *('e-OH-no)* . . . . Six

EHIKU *('e-HEE-ku)* . . . . . . Seven

EWALU *('e-VAH-lu)* . . . . . . Eight

EIWA *('AY-va)* . . . . Nine

UMI *('OO-mi)* . . . . Ten

YOUR BIRTHDAY MONTH – IN HAWAIIAN!

IANUALI *(ya-nu-WAH-li)* . . . . January
PEPELUALI *(pe-pe-lu-WAH-li)* . . . . . . February
MALAKI *(ma-LAH-ki)* . . . . March
APELILA *('a-pe-LEE-la)* . . . . April
MEI *(MAY)* . . . . May
IUNE *(YOO-ne)* . . . . June
IULAI *(yu-LEYE)* . . . . July
AUKAKE *('ow-KAH-ke)* . . . . August
KEPAKEMAPA *(ke-pa-ke-MAH-pa)* . . September
OKAKOPA *('o-ka-KOH-pa)* . . . . October
NOWEMAPA *(no-we-MAH-pa)* . . . . . . November
KEKEMAPA *(ke-ke-MAH-pa)* . . . . December

DAYS OF THE WEEK – IN HAWAIIAN!

POAKAHI *(po-wa-KAH-hi)* . . . . Monday
POALUA *(po-wa-LOO-wa)* . . . . Tuesday
POAKOLU *(po-wa-KOH-lu)* . . . . Wednesday
POAHA *(po-WAH-ha)* . . . . Thursday
POALIMA *(po-wa-LEE-ma)* . . . . Friday
POAONO *(po-wa-OH-no)* . . . . Saturday
LAPULE *(la-POO-le)* . . . . Sunday

THE TIME OF DAY – THE HAWAIIAN WAY

WANA'AO *(wa-na-'OW)* . . . . Dawn
KAKAHIAKA *(ka-ka-hi-YAH-ka)* . . . . Morning
AWAKEA *(a-wa-KEH-ya)* . . . . Noon
AUINALA *(ow-wi-na-LAH)* . . . . Afternoon
AHIAHI *(a-hi-YAH-hi)* . . . . Evening
POLEHULEHU *(po-LEH-hu-LEH-hu)* . . Dusk
PO *(POH)* . . . . Dark night
AUMOE *(OW-MOY)* . . . . Midnight

SEASONS OF THE YEAR – IN HAWAIIAN!

KUPULAU *(KOO-pu-LOW)* . . . . Spring
KAU WELA *(KOW-WEH-la)* . . . . Summer
HA'ULE LAU *(ha-'OO-le LOW)* . . . . Fall
HO'OILO *(HOH-'o-EE-lo)* . . . . Winter

KUPULAU

IN HAWAIIAN KNOW ...
YOUR HEAD TO TOE!

'A'I ('AH-'EE) . . . . Neck
ALELO (a-LEH-lo) . . . . Tongue
'AUWAE ('ow-WEYE) . . . . Chin
HANU (HAH-nu) . . . . Breath
HELELHELENA (HEH-le-he-LEH-na) . . Face
HILA (HEE-la) . . . . Heel
IHU ('EE-hu) . . . . Nose
'ILI ('EE-li) . . . . Skin
'I'O ('EE-'o) . . . . Muscle
'IWI ('EE-vi) . . . . Bone
'IWI 'AO 'AO ('EE-vi 'OW 'OW) . . . . Rib
KIKALA (ki-KAH-la) . . . . Hip

KINO (KEE-no) . . . . Body
KOKO (KOH-ko) . . . . Blood
KUA (KOO-wa) . . . . Back
KU'EKU'E LIMA (KOO-'e-KOO-'e LEE-ma) . . . . Elbow
KU'EKU'E MAKA (KOO-'e-KOO-'e MAH-ka) . . . . Eyebrows
KU'EKU'E WAWAE (KOO-'e-KOO-'e WAH-weye) . . . . Ankle
KULI (KOO-li) . . . . Knee
LAUOHO (low-OH-ho) . . . . Hair
LEHELEHE (LEH-he-LEH-he) . . . . Lips
LIHILIHIMAKA (LEE-hi-LEE-hi-MAH-ka) . . . . Eyelids
LIMA (LEE-ma) . . . . Arm, hand
LOLO (LOH-lo) . . . . Brain
MAKA (MAH-ka) . . . . Eye
MANAMANA LIMA (MAH-na-MAH-na LEE-ma) . . . . Finger
MANAMANA LIMA NUI (MAH-na-MAH-na LEE-ma NOO-wi) . . .Thumb
MANAMANAWAWAE (MAH-na-MAH-na-WAH-WEYE) . . . . Toe
NIHO (NEE-ho) . . . . Tooth
OKOLE (o-KOH-le) . . . . Posterior
OPU (o-POO) . . . . Stomach
PAPALINA (pa-pa-LEE-na) . . . . Cheek
PEPEIAO (pe-pe-YOW) . . . . Ear
PIKO (PEE-ko) . . . . Navel
POLI (POH-li) . . . . Bosom
PO'O (POH-'o) . . . . Head
PO'OHIWI (POH-'o-HEE-vi) . . . . Shoulder
PUHAKA (pu-HAH-ka) . . . . Waist
PU'U (POO-'u) . . . . Throat

PUʻUWAI *(POO-ʻu-WEYE)* .... Heart
ʻUHA *(ʻOO-ha)* .... Thigh
ʻUMAUMA *(ʻu-MOW-ma)* .... Chest
WAHA *(WAH-ha)* .... Mouth
WAWAE *(wa-WEYE)* .... Leg, Foot

THE WHAT 'N WHERE 'N WHY FOR IN HAWAIIAN

ʻEHIA *(ʻe-HEE-ya)*
How many?

ʻEHIA KO KEIA
(ʻe-HEE-ya ko ke-EE-ya)
How much is this one?

HE AHA *(he AH-ha)*
What?

HE AHA HOU AIE
(he AH-ha HOH AH-ʻe)
What next? What else?

HEWA PAHA *(HEH-va PAH-ha)*
Is it wrong?

HOLA ʻEHIA KEIA
(HOH-la ʻe-HEE-ya ke-EE-ya)
What time is it?

I KA WA HEA
(EE ka wa HEH-a)
When?

HE AHA HOU AIE

24

HAWAII'S TOASTS, GREETINGS, ENDEARMENTS, SALUTATIONS!

A HUI HOU KAUA
(a HOO-i HOH-u ka-OO-wa)
Until we meet again.

ALOHA *(a-LOH-ha)*
Welcome, love, affection, hello, good-bye.

ALOHA AHIAHI *(a-LOH-ha AH-hi-YAH-hi)*
Good evening.

ALOHA AU IA OE *(a-LOH-ha OW EE-ya 'OY)*
I love you.

ALOHA AUINALA *(a-LOH-ha OW-EE-na-la)*
Good afternoon.

ALOHA KAKAHIAKA
(a-LOH-ha ka-ka-hi-YAH-ka)
Good morning.

ALOHA KAKOU *(a-LOH-ha ka-KOH)*
Congratulations! Greetings!

ALOHA NUI *(a-LOH-ha NOO-wi)*
A big aloha!

ALOHA NUI LOA *(a-LOH-ha NOO-wi LOH-wa)*
Much love to you.

ALOHA NUI KAKOU *(a-LOH-ha NOO-i ka-KOH)*
Greetings or love to all including myself! (More intimate)

ALOHA OUKOU *(a-LOH-ha OH-u-KOH)*
Greetings of love to all of you.

HAUOLI LA HANAU *(how-'OH-li la ha-NOW)*
Happy Birthday!

HAUOLI MAKAHIKI HOU *(how-'OH-li ma-ka-HEE-ki HOH)*
Happy New Year!

HAUOLI MAOLI OE *(how-'OH-li MOW-li OY)*
Here's to your happiness!

KA HANA MA'A MAU O KA AINA
(ka HAH-na MA-'a MOW o ka EYE-na)
The courtesies of the Land.

ALOHA KAKOU

HAPPY NEW YEAR!

MELE KALIKIMAKA

KAMAU *(ka-MOW)*
Here's how! Here's to your health!

KANIKAPILA *(KAH-ni-ka-PEE-la)*
Strike up the music!

KIPA MAI *(KEE-pa MEYE)*
Welcome.

KOMO *(KOH-mo)*
Enter.

MAHALO *(ma-HAH-lo)*
Thank you; Thanks.

MAHALO NUI *(ma-HAH-lo NOO-i)*
Many thanks.

MAHALO NUI LOA
(ma-HAH-lo NOO-i LOH-a)
Thank you very much.

MAHOPE *(ma-HOH-pe)*
Later.

MAI HELE 'OE *(MEYE he-le 'OY)*
Don't go.

MAIKA'I *(meye KAH-'i)*
Fine.

MAIKA'I NO *(meye-KAH-'i NOH)*
Very fine.

MAI MAKA'U *(MEYE ma-KAH-'u)*
Don't be afraid.

MAI MOLOWA *(MEYE mo-lo-WAH)*
Don't be lazy.

MAI POINA *(MEYE POY-na)*
Don't forget.

MAKE WAI AU
(MAH-ke weye yow)
I'm thirsty.

MALAMA PONO
(ma-LAH-ma POH-no)
Be careful.

MALUHILUHI AU
(MAH-LOO-hi-LOO-hi yow)
I'm tired.

OKOLE MALUNA

NUI KA WELA!

MALUNA, MALALO, MAWAENA
(ma-LOO-na, ma-LAH-lo, ma-va-EE-na)
As you toast, you touch glasses at
"The top, the bottom, and the middle."
In other words, "All and every way."

MAOPOPO IA'U
(MOW-po-po YAH-'u)
I understand.

ME KE ALOHA *(me ke a-LOH-ha)*
With love.

ME KE ALOHA PAU OLE
(me ke a-LOH-ha pow 'OH-le)
With love or good wishes without end.

MELE KALIKIMAKA
(MEH-le ka-LEE-ki-MAH-ka)
Merry Christmas.

MINAMINA *(MEE-na-MEE-na)*
How regrettable.

NANA'OE *(NAH-NAH-'OY)*
Look!

NANI WAHINE *(NAH-ni wa-HEE-ne)*
To a beautiful women.

NOHO 'OE *(NOH-ho 'OY)*
Stay; sit.

NO KA OI *(no ka 'OY)*
Best of all.

NO KE ALOHA *(no ke a-LOH-ha)*
For love.

NUI KA WELA *(NOO-i ka VEH-la)*
Very hot.

OKOLE MALUNA
(o-KOH-le ma-LOO-na)
Bottoms up!

OLU'OLU *('OH-lu 'OH-lu)*
Please.

PAU *(POW)*
Finished.

PEHEA ‘OE *(pe-HEH-a ‘OY)*
How do you do?

PELA KU‘U MANA‘O
(PEH-la KOO-‘u ma-NAH-‘o)
I suppose so.

PELA PAHA, ‘A ‘OLE PAHA
(PEH-la PAH-ha, ‘AH ‘OH-le PAH-ha)
Maybe so, maybe not.

PIPII LOA *(pi-PEE-‘i LOH-a)*
Too much! Very expensive!

POLOLEI *(po-lo-LAY)*
That's all right!

POLOLI AU *(POH-LOH-li yow)*
I'm hungry.

PONO *(POH-no)*
Right!

PONO NO ‘OE *(POH-no no ‘OY)*
You're so right!

PUPULE KELA
(pu-POO-le KEH-LAH)
That's crazy!

UA PONO NO *(u-wa POH-no NOH)*
It is right!

WELA KA HAO *(WEH-la ka HOW)*
Whoopee! Let's have fun! Strike
while the iron is hot!

A HUI HOU KAUA (UNTIL WE MEET AGAIN)

28

ISLAND FASHIONS
YOU'LL SEE EVERYWHERE
ON EVERYONE!!!

ALOHA SHIRT *(a-LOH-ha)*
Hawaiian-English description of an
Hawaiian designed, brightly colored shirt.
Worn without a tie and usually open at
the neck, it is considered informal attire
for men.

"BLOCKED" DENIM
Derived from English words. A block
denim type of fabric originally used to
make plantation shirts and other garments.

HOLOKU *(ho-lo-KOO)*
A woman's long formal gown with a train.

KEKEPA *(ke-KEH-pa)*
A wrap around garment commonly used in ancient
times. Often seen on hula dancers today.

MALO *(MAH-lo)*
The loin cloth worn by males.

MUUMUU *(MOO-u-MOO-u)*
Hawaii's Mother Hubbard, the full length dress brought about through
missionary influence. Today's design is geared to the ease and comfort of
casual island living.

ALOHA SHORTS

SHORTIE MUU

SHORTY MUU *(MOO-'u)*
Dress length version of the muumuu.

MANDARIN MUU *(pronounced as appears)*
This muumuu, adapted with Chinese
style influences, has a high collar,
side seams slashed to the knee and a
slim tapered line.

PALAKA *(pa-LAH-ka)*
A block-print Hawaiian shirt
that is a favorite for all ages.

PAPALE *(pa-PAH-le)*
A hat or bonnet.

PRINCESS MUUMU

PA'U *(PAH-'u)*
Also pau pau. This sarong is worn by the Polynesian
women and especially by dancers today.

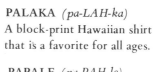

PAKE MUU

The Afro-muu, the Pagoda style muu
and the Kabuki are examples of design
innovations that were created by ethnic
influences. Style changes are reflected
in the Empire line, the Princess style and
the Shorty muu.

AMI *('AH-mi)*
A hula step of hip rotations.

HAINA *(HAH-'EE-na)*
Gesture that shows end of hula dance; right foot pointed forward, arms extended, hands held together, palms to audience.

HANA HOU *(HAH-na HOH-u)*
To do it again; repeat, encore.

HELA *(HEH-la)*
Hula step; the pointing of foot forward and outward.

HOULIULI *(HOH-'OO-li-'OO-li)*
To shake the Uliuli.

HULA *(HOO-la)*
The art of Hawaiian dance.

IPU *('EE-pu)*
Hula instrument; hollow gourd which has varying sounds when hit by parts of the hand or on the ground.

ILI ILI *('EE-li 'EE-li)*
Used when dancing the hula; small stones which are clicked two in each hand.

HULA

KALAAU PU ILI   ILI ILI   IPU   ULI ULI

31

KALAAU *(ka-la-'OW)*
Hard wooden sticks that make varying sounds
when hit together.

ONI ONI
('OH-ni 'OH-ni)
To wiggle; to move.

PU ILI *(pu 'EE-li)*
Another hula accompaniment; made
of split bamboo.

UKULELE *('OO-ku-LEH-le)*
Small guitar, meaning "jumping flea".

ULILI *('u-LEE-li)*
A gyrating/rotating musical instrument consisting
of three gourds pierced by a stick.

'ULI 'ULI *('u-LEE 'u-LEE)*
A rattling gourd; gourd contains seeds and has colored
feathers at the top.

UWEHE *('u-WEH-he)*
Hula step; knee and foot movements.

UKULELE

ONI ONI

HAWAII'S FLOWERS, PLANTS, TREES, FRUITS, VEGETABLES — KNOW THEM BY SIGHT AND NAME!

AKAAKAI *('a-KAH-'a-KEYE)*
Onion.

AKALA *(a-KAH-la)*
Endemic raspberry.

AKULIKULI *(a-KOO-li-KOO-li)*
Small aster-like flower with bright rose-colored petals used for leis.

ALOALO *(AH-lo-AH-lo)*
Hibiscus; Hawaii's official State Flower.

ALOALO

APE *(AH-pe)*
These flowers are up to a foot long. The elephant ear type leaves are very large and grow from 4 to 5 feet. Ape is related to the taro plant species.

AWA PUHI *('a-va POO-hi)*
The torch ginger flower.

HALA *(HAH-la)*
Pandanus tree; leaves used for weaving.

HAU *(HOW)*
A spreading tree.

HUA *(HOO-wa)*
Fruit, seed.

HUAPALA *(HOO-wa-PAH-la)*
Meaning "Sweetheart", this is the Orange Trumpet Vine. It has long, slender tube-type flame flowers with 4 to 5 lobes which curl back.

APE

HUAWAINA *(Hoo-wa-WEYE-na)*
Grape.

ILIAHI *('EE-li-'AH-hi)*
Sandalwood.

ILIMA *(i-LEE-ma)*
The Royal Hawaiian flower; gold-orange or white.

IPU HAOLE *('EE-pu HOW-le)*
Watermelon.

KAMANI *(ka-MAH-ni)*
A Hawaiian tree.

KIAWE *(ki-YAH-ve)*
Algaroba tree.

AWA PuHi

KIKA *(KEE-KAH)*
Cigar flower. Used for leis.
Flowers are orange-red or white.

KOA *(KOH-wa)*
A large native forest tree, Koa means "brave warrior."

KOU *(KOH-u)*
Large shade tree.

KUKUI *(ku-KOO-i)*
A candlenut tree.

KUMULA'AU *(KOO-mu-la-'OW)*
Tree.

LANí-ALii

LANI-ALII *(LAH-ni a-LEE-'i)*
Meaning "Heavenly Chief", this is the Yellow Allamanda.

LAU *(LOW)*
Leaf.

LAUHALA *(LOW-HAH-la)*
Pandanus leaf.

LEHUA *(le-HOO-wa)*
A Hawaiian flower. Red, and like a powder puff.

LEI *(LAY)*
Flower necklace, garland.

LOKE *(LOH-ke)*
Rose.

LOULU *(LOH-u-lu)*
Native palm.

HUAPALA

MAI'A *(MEYE-'a)*
Banana.

MAILE *(MEYE-le)*
A vine.

MALA *(MAH-la)*
Garden.

MAUNALOA *(MOW-na-LOH-wa)*
Wild pea vine with lavendar, white or maroon flowers. Used for leis.

MILIKANA *(mi-li-KAH-na)*
Papaya.

NAHELE *(na-HEH-le)*
Forest.

LEHUA HAOLE

NANA HONUA *(NAH-NAH ho-NOO-wa)*
Meaning "Gazing Earthward," this is the Angel's
Trumpet, a bell-shaped flower that blossoms in the
thousands on trees. Usually flowers are white,
but sometimes lavendar and pale salmon in color.

NAUPAKA *(NOW-PAH-ka)*
Beach bush with ½ flowers.

NANA HONUA

NIU *(NEE-yu)*
Coconut.

OHAI *('o-HEYE)*
Monkey-pod.

OHE *('o-HEH)*
Bamboo.

OHIA LEHUA *('o-HEE-'a le-HOO-wa)*
Pele's flower of the Ohia Tree used for leis in ancient days.

PAKALANA *(pa-ka-LAH-na)*
Chinese violet.

PANINI O KAPUNAHOU *(pa-NEE-ni o ka-POO-na-HOH)*
Referred to as the flower of Heaven and Earth,
this is the fabulous Night-blooming Cereus
which blossoms only at night.

PANINI-O-KAPUNAHOU

PAPAPA *(pa-PAH-pa)*
Bean.

PIKAKE *(pi-KAH-ke)*
The Chinese Jasmine in Hawaii; its name is a corrupt
English word "Peacock", so called because it was
the flower of Princess Kaiulani, identified with her peacocks.

PILI *(PEE-li)*
Thatching grass.

PILIKAI *(PEE-li-KEYE)*
Wood rose.

MELIA

POHA *(po-HAH)*
Cape Gooseberry.

POHUEHUE *(po-HOO-e-HOO-e)*
Beach vine.

PONIMOI *(POH-ni-MOY)*
Carnation.

PU *(POO)*
Squash.

PUA *(POO-wa)*
Flower, blossom.

PUAKALA *(POO-wa-KAH-la)*
Prickly poppy (Beach poppy).

PUA KENIKENI *(POO-wa KEH-ni-KEH-ni)*
Fragrant, waxy flower used for leis.

PUALELE *(POO-wa-LEH-le)*
Dandelion.

PUA MALE *(POO-wa MAH-le)*
Stephanotis, white marriage flower.

PUMELI *(POO-MEH-li)*
    or **MELIA** *(me-LEE-ya)*
A popular lei flower, known better
as the Plumeria, this fragrant periwinkle
flower belongs to the Frangipani family.

TI *(TEE)*
Correctly, the Hawaiian Ki *(KEE)* plant.

UALA KAHIKI *('u-WAH-la ka-HEE-ki)*
Irish potato.

UALA MAOLI *('u-WAH-la MOW-li)*
Sweet potato.

ULU *('OO-'lu)*
Breadfruit.

WILIWILI *(WEE-li-WEE-li)*
A tree.

OFFICIAL LEI OF
EACH HAWAIIAN ISLAND

HINAHINA *(HEE-na-HEE-na)* — KAHOOLAWE

Silvery-Grey Lei. Originally beach heliotrope was used, but it is hard to find. Spanish Moss of silvery grey hues is now used for this Lei of the uninhabited "target island" of Kahoolawe.

ILIMA *('i-LEE-ma)* — OAHU

Orange-Yellow Lei. The flower of Royalty, the Ilima is used for the Lei representing the Capital Isle of Oahu.

KAUNAOA *(KOW-na-'OH-wa)* — LANAI

Orange Lei. A peculiar plant with bright orange thread-like stems, no leaves and sometimes tiny inconspicuous flowers, make up this Lei for the Pineapple Isle of Lanai.

KUKUI *(ku-KOO-wi)* — MOLOKAI

Silvery-Green Lei. The tiny clustered ivory-white flowers and silvery green leaves of the Kukui (Candlenut) Tree are used for the Lei of the Friendly Isle of Molokai.

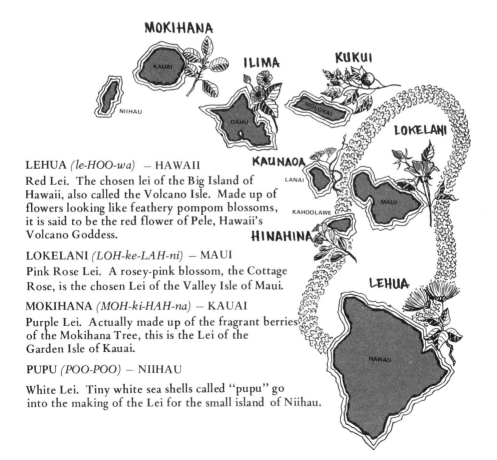

LEHUA *(le-HOO-wa)* — HAWAII

Red Lei. The chosen lei of the Big Island of Hawaii, also called the Volcano Isle. Made up of flowers looking like feathery pompom blossoms, it is said to be the red flower of Pele, Hawaii's Volcano Goddess.

LOKELANI *(LOH-ke-LAH-ni)* — MAUI

Pink Rose Lei. A rosey-pink blossom, the Cottage Rose, is the chosen Lei of the Valley Isle of Maui.

MOKIHANA *(MOH-ki-HAH-na)* — KAUAI

Purple Lei. Actually made up of the fragrant berries of the Mokihana Tree, this is the Lei of the Garden Isle of Kauai.

PUPU *(POO-POO)* — NIIHAU

White Lei. Tiny white sea shells called "pupu" go into the making of the Lei for the small island of Niihau.

HAWAII'S RAINBOW OF COLORS

AHINAHINA *('a-HEE-na-HEE-na)* . . . . Gray
AKALA *(a-KAH-la)* . . . . Pink
ALANI *('a-LAH-ni)* . . . . Orange
ELEELE *('EH-le-'EH-le)* . . . . Black
HUAPALA *(HOO-wa-PAH-la)* . . . . Chestnut
KALAKOA *(KAH-la-KOH-wa)* . . . . Calico
KIKOKIKO *(KEE-ko-KEE-ko)* . . . . Spotted
KEOKEO *(KEH-'o-KEH-'o)* . . . . White
LENA *(LEH-na)* . . . . Yellow
OMA OMA 'O *('OH-MAH 'o-MAH 'o)* . . . . Green
POLU *(po-LOO)* . . . . Blue
PONI *(POH-ni)* . . . . Purple
ULAULA *('OO-la-'OO-la)* . . . . Red

THE NATURE OF THINGS IN HAWAII

A'A *(AH-'AH)* . . . . Rough lava

AHI *(AH-hi)* . . . . Fire

ANA *(AH-na)* . . . . Cave

ANUENUE *(AH-NOO-we-NOO-we)* . . . . Rainbow

AO *(OW)* . . . . World

AOULI *(ow-OO-li)* . . . . Sky

EA *(EH-ya)* . . . . Air

HEKILI *(he-KEE-li)* . . . . Thunder

HOKU *(HOH-ku)* . . . . Star

HOKULELE *(HOH-ku-LEH-le)* . . . . Meteor

HONUA *(ho-NOO-wa)* . . . . Earth

'INO'INO *('EE-no-'EE-no)* . . . . Storm

KAHAWAI *(ka-ha-WEYE)* . . . . Stream

KAI *(KEYE)* . . . . Sea water

KI'OWAI *(KEE-'o-WEYE)* . . . . Pool

LA *(LAH)* . . . . Sun

LANI *(LAH-ni)* . . . . Heaven

LEPO *(LEH-po)* . . . . Dirt, soil

LUAPELE *(LOO-wa-PEH-le)* . . . . Volcano
MAHINA *(ma-HEE-na)* . . . . Moon
MIMILO *(mi-MEE-lo)* . . . . Whirlpool
MOANA *(mo-WAH-na)* . . . . Ocean
NAULU *(na-OO-lu)* . . . . Sudden rain
OHU *('OH-hu)* . . . . Fog
OLA'I *('o-LAH-'i)* . . . . Earthquake
ONE *('OH-ne)* . . . . Sand
PAHOEHOE *(pa-HOY-HOY)* . . . . Smooth lava
PO *(POH)* . . . . Night
POHAKU *(po-HAH-ku)* . . . . Stone, rock
PUNAWAI *(POO-na-WEYE)* . . . . Spring
PU'U *(POO-'u)* . . . . Hill
UA *(OO-wa)* . . . . Rain
UAHI *('u-WAH-hi)* . . . . Smoke
UILA *('u-WEE-la)* . . . . Lightning
WAI *(WEYE)* . . . . Fresh water
WAILELE *(WEYE-le-le)* . . . . Waterfall

PELE, HAWAII'S VOLCANO GODDESS DESCRIBES HER "LAVA HOLDINGS" HAWAII'S VOLCANOES

PELE *(PEH-le)*

According to ancient Hawaiian legend, Pele is the Goddess of Hawaii's Volcanoes.

Hawaii is said to be the only place in the world where spectators rush toward the scene of an erupting volcano instead of away from it. The old Hawaiian people called a volcano eruption "Alealea" *(AH-le-ya-LEH-ya)* "the greatest of entertainment." The Hawaiian Islands are actually the tops of a range of mighty mountains, most likely the greatest mountain range on earth, built up from the sea floor by thousands of volcanic eruptions.

KILAUEA *(ki-low-WAY-ya)*
(On the Big Island of Hawaii)

Meaning "Rising Smoke Cloud," Kilauea is the most active of the world's volcanic mountains. A shield volcano, its summit stands about 20,000 feet above the surrounding ocean floor. The summit caldera, or crater, of Kilauea is 2½ miles long and 2 miles wide and its floor has an area of 2,600 acres.

MAUNA LOA *(MOW-na LOH-wa)*
(On the Big Island of Hawaii)

This volcano, meaning "Long Mountain," is in South Kona, Hawaii. A shield volcano, Mauna Loa is the world's largest active volcano and probably the largest single mountain of any sort on earth. It rises 13,680 feet above sea level and approximately 30,000 feet above its base at the ocean floor. Its crater, Mokuaweoweo *(MOH-ku-wa-WEH-yo-WEH-yo)*, is approximately 3 miles long and 1½ miles wide.

HALEAKALA *(HAH-le-a-ka-la)*
(On the Island of Maui)

One of the world's most active volcanoes, Haleakala, "The House of the Sun," contains many small craters. It is a big volcanic mountain, built up from the ocean floor to an altitude of 8,000 feet above the present sea level to form the eastern part of the island of Maui. Haleakala is the only volcano in the Hawaiian group, except on the island of Hawaii, that has erupted during the last few hundred years.

HALEMAUMAU *(HAH-le-MOW-MOW)*
(On the Big Island of Hawaii)

The "Fire Pit," Halemaumau, a collapsed crater about 32,000 feet wide and over 500 feet deep within the summit caldera, is the principal vent of Kilauea Volcano. Halemaumau is the focus of Kilauea's eruptions and the traditional home of Madame Pele.

MAUNA KEA *(MOW-na KEH-ya)*
(On the Big Island of Hawaii)

This volcano, meaning "White Mountain," is in Hamakua on the island of Hawaii. A dormant volcano, Mauna Kea rises about 30,000 to 32,000 feet above its base. It is the highest peak in the islands and quite probably the world's highest mountain in terms of elevation above its base.

KILAUEA IKI *(ki-low-WAY-ya EE-ki)*
(On the Big Island of Hawaii)

Meaning "Little Kilauea," Kilauea Iki is a pit crater immediately adjacent to the eastern edge of Kilauea Caldera. During one of its eruptions, it shot a fountain of lava 1,900 feet into the air, more than 500 feet higher than the Empire State Building.

KOHALA *(ko-HAH-la)*
(On the Big Island of Hawaii)

Named after the "Pandanus Tree," Kohala is one of the five great volcanoes that built the Big Island of Hawaii. It is older than Mauna Kea and rises 5,505 feet above sea level. Now extinct, it is covered with old cinder cones and has deep valleys cut into it on the windward side.

PAHOEHOE *(pa-HOY-HOY)*

Pahoehoe lava has a smooth ropey or glassy surface. Frequently, the skin or crust of Pahoehoe lava wrinkles or pushes together, forming a surface looking like ropes laid side by side and at other times like rock pillows. Pahoehoe can flow 35 miles an hour down a steep slope.

A'A *(AH'AH)*

Melted lava rock that is less fluid than Pahoehoe is called A'a. It has a very rough, spiny, clinkery or tubbly surface with a massive interior. A fast A'a flow may move as much as 100 feet in one hour. When it pushes in the ocean, A'a makes the sea boil and steam. Some of the A'a explodes into glassy black sand that washes along the shore. The famous black sand beaches on Hawaii, at Punaluu and Kalapana, are the result of such A'a action.

KIPUKA *(kee-POO-ka)*

An "island" of old land with a lava flow, Kipuka means "an opening".

PELE'S HAIR *(PEH-le)*

Volcanic glass spun out into hairlike form is referred to as the hair of Hawaii's volcano goddess, Pele.

PELE'S TEARS *(PEH-le)*

Congealed lava droplets, supposedly Pele's.

HUALALAI *(HOO-wa-la-LEYE)*

On the western side of the Big Island, Hualalai was believed to have been quiet for a long time until it erupted in 1801. It hasn't been active since.

THE 4-MAJOR AKUA TIKI GOD IMAGES OF ANCIENT HAWAII

KANALOA   KANE   KU   LONO

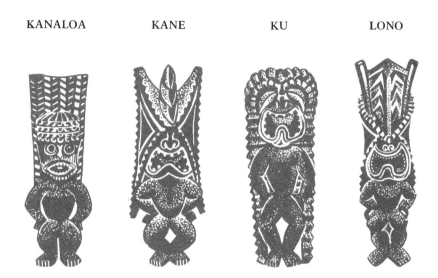

KANALOA *(ka-na-LOH-wa)*
One of the four major gods of ancient Polynesia, Kanaloa was said to be the god of the ocean depths and land of departed spirits. He has been endowed with strong and weak human traits, and considered the eternal god. Today, Kanaloa is referred to as the god of eternal hope and guidance, bestowing understanding between all men and promising eternal happiness.

KANE *(KAH-ne)*
The leading god among the four great gods of ancient Hawaii, Kane was a god of creation and the ancestor of chiefs and commoners; a god of sunlight, fresh water and forests, to whom no human sacrifices were made. Today, Kane is looked to as the creator god of life and light promising the ultimate in health and happiness.

KU *(KOO)*
Ku, also one of the four major gods of ancient Hawaii, represented male generating power and was known as the god of war. When gathering medicine with their right hands, people prayed to Ku for success. Today, Ku is said to be the protector god who wards off war through the force of his fierce image. Ku ruled the people's destiny through his influence on their leaders.

LONO *(LOH-no)*
The most revered of the four great gods of old Hawaii, Lono was the supreme god of peace and fertility. He was considered a god of clouds, winds, the sea, agriculture, and fertility. He was the patron of the annual harvest "Makahiki" festival. Today, Lono is looked to as the god of peace and prosperity, offering the promise of a wealth of life's blessings.

FIND YOUR NAME IN HAWAIIAN, IF WAHINE*

API	*(AH-pi)*	ABBIE
APIKA'ILA	*(a-PEE-ka-'EE-la)*	ABIGAIL
AKA	*(AH-ka)*	ADA
AKELAIKA	*(a-ke-LEYE-ka)*	ADELAIDE
AKELINA	*(a-ke-LEE-na)*	ADELINE
AKAKA	*(a-KAH-ka)*	AGATHA
AKENEKI	*(a-ke-NEH-ki)*	AGNES
AILINA	*(EYE-LEE-na)*	AILENE
ALEPEKA	*(a-le-PEH-ka)*	ALBERTA
ALEKA	*(a-LEH-ka)*	ALICE

*WAHINE *(wa-HEE-ne)* — Female.

45

ALEMA . . . . (a-LEH-ma) . . . . ALMA
ALAWINA . . . . (a-la-VEE-na) . . . . ALVINA
AMANAKA . . . . (a-ma-NAH-ka) . . . . AMANDA
EME . . . . (EH-me) . . . . AMY
ANAKALIA . . . . (a-na-ka-LEE-ya) . . . . ANDREA
ANELA . . . . (a-NEH-la) . . . . ANGELA
ANIKA . . . . (a-NEE-ka) . . . . ANITA
ANA . . . . (AH-na) . . . . ANN(E), ANNA
ANAPELA . . . . (a-na-PEH-la) . . . . ANNABELLE
ANEKA . . . . (a-NEH-ka) . . . . ANNETTE
ANE . . . . (AH-ne) . . . . ANNIE
AUKELE . . . . (OW-KEH-le) . . . . AUDREY
PALAPALA . . . . (PAH-la-PAH-la) . . . . BARBARA
PEAKALIKA . . . . (pe-a-ka-LEE-ka) . . . . BEATRICE
PEKE . . . . (PEH-ke) . . . . BECKY
PELA . . . . (PEH-la) . . . . BELLA, BELLE
PELENAKEKA . . . . . (pe-le-na-KEH-ka) . . . . BERNADETTE
PELENAKINO . . . . . (PEH-le-na-KEE-no) . . . . . . BERNADINE
PELENIKE . . . . (PEH-le-NEE-ki) . . . . BERNICE
PELEKA . . . . (pe-LEH-ka) . . . . BERTHA
PELULO . . . . (pe-LOO-lo) . . . . BERYL
ELIKAPEKA . . . . (e-LEE-ka-PEH-ka) . . . . BETH
PEKE . . . . (PEH-ke) . . . . BETTY
PONI . . . . (POH-ni) . . . . BONNIE
PALANEKE . . . . (PAH-la-NEH-ke) . . . . BLANCHE
PILIKIKA . . . . (pi-li-KEE-ka) . . . . BRIGET
KALOKA . . . . (ka-LOH-ka) . . . . CARLOTTA
KALAMELA . . . . (ka-la-MEH-la) . . . . CARMEN
KALOLA . . . . (ka-LOH-la) . . . . CAROL
KALOLAINA . . . . . . (KAH-lo-LEYE-na) . . . . CAROLINE
KAKALINA . . . . (KAH-ka-LEE-na) . . . . CATHERINE
KIKILIA . . . . (ki-ki-LEE-ya) . . . . CECELIA
HALAKI . . . . (ha-LAH-ki) . . . . CHARLOTTE
KILIKINA . . . . (ki-li-KEE-na) . . . . CHRISTINA(E)
KALEA . . . . (ka-LEH-ya) . . . . CLAIRE
KALALA . . . . (ka-LAH-la) . . . . CLARA
KALALIKA . . . . (ka-la-LEE-ka) . . . . CLARICE
KALAUKINA . . . . (ka-low-KEE-na) . . . . CLAUDINE
KOLINA . . . . (ko-LEE-na) . . . . CORRINNE
KINIKIA . . . . (KEE-ni-KEE-ya) . . . . CYNTHIA
KEPOLA . . . . (ke-POH-la) . . . . DEBORAH

KIANA	(ki-AH-na)	DIANA
KINA	(KEE-na)	DINAH
KOLOLEKE	(ko-lo-LEH-ke)	DOLORES
KOLA	(KOH-la)	DORA
KOLINA	(ko-LEE-na)	DOREEN
KOLIKA	(ko-LEE-ka)	DORIS
KOLOKEA	(KOH-lo-KEH-ya)	DOROTHY
EKIKA	(e-KEE-ka)	EDITH
EKENA	(e-KEH-na)	EDNA
AILINA	(eye-LEE-na)	EILENE
ILEINA	(i-LAY-na)	ELAINE
ELENOLA	(EH-le-NOH-la)	ELEANOR
ELIKAPEKA	(e-LEE-ka-PEH-ka)	ELIZABETH
ELA	(EH-la)	ELLA
ELENA	(e-LEH-na)	ELLEN
ELOIKA	(e-lo-WEE-ka)	ELOISE
ELEKI	(e-LEH-ki)	ELSIE
EMELE	(e-me-LEH)	EMILY
EMA	(EH-ma)	EMMA
ELIKA	(e-LEE-ka)	ERICA
ELENEKINA	(e-le-ne-KEE-na)	ERNESTINE
EKEKELA	(e-ke-KEH-la)	ESTELLE, ESTHER
EKELA	(e-KEH-la)	ETHEL
IUKINIA	(yu-ki-NEE-ya)	EUGENIA
EUNIKE	(yu-NEE-ke)	EUNICE
IWA	(EE-va)	EVA
EWA	(EH-va)	EVE
EWALINA	(e-va-LEE-na)	EVELYN
MANA'O'I'O	(ma-NAH-'o-'EE-'o)	FAITH
PANE	(PAH-ne)	FANNY
POLOLA	(po-LOH-la)	FLORA
POLOLENA	(po-lo-LEH-na)	FLORENCE
PALAKIKA	(pa-la-KEE-ka)	FRANCES
KAILA	(KEYE-la)	GAIL
KEOKIANA	(KEH-yo-ki-YAH-na)	GEORGIANA
KEOKINA	(KEH-yo-KEE-na)	GEORGINA
KEOKIA	(KEH-yo-KEE-ya)	GEORGIA
KEKALUKA	(KEH-ka-LOO-ka)	GERTRUDE
KOLOLIA	(ko-lo-LEE-ya)	GLORIA
KALEKI	(ka-LEH-ki)	GRACE

HANA	(HAH-na)	HANNAH
HALIAKA	(HAH-li-YAH-ka)	HARRIET
HAKELA	(ha-KEH-la)	HAZEL
HELENA	(he-LEH-na)	HELEN
HENELIAKA	(he-ne-li-YAH-ka)	HENRIETTA
HEKEKELA	(he-ke-KEH-la)	HESTER
HILEKA	(hi-LEH-ka)	HILDA
MANA 'OLANA	(ma-NAH-'o-LAH-na)	HOPE
AIKA	(EYE-ka)	IDA
AINA	(EYE-na)	INA
AINEKI	(EYE-NEH-ki)	INEZ
AILINA	(EYE-LEE-na)	IRENE
IKAPELA	(EE-ka-PEH-la)	ISABELLE
KINI	(KEE-ni)	JANE, JEAN, JENNIE
KEAKALINA	(KEH-ya-ka-LEE-na)	JACQUELINE
IANEKE	(ya-NEH-ke)	JANET, JANETTE
IOANA	(yo-WAH-na)	JOAN, JOANNE
IOKEPINE	(yo-ke-PEE-ne)	JOSEPHINE
WANIKA	(wa-NEE-ka)	JUANITA
IUKIKA	(yu-KEE-ka)	JUDITH
IULIA	(YOO-li-ya)	JULIA
KULIANA	(ku-li-AH-na)	JULIETTE
IUNE	(YOO-ne)	JUNE
KEKE	(KEH-ke)	KATE, KATIE
KAKALINA	(ka-ka-LEE-na)	KATHERINE
KAKALINE	(ka-ka-LEE-ne)	KATHLEEN
LALA	(LAH-la)	LAURA
LINA	(LEE-na)	LENA
LEONOLA	(le-yo-NOH-la)	LEONORA
LILIANA	(li-li-AH-na)	LILLIAN
LILIA	(li-LEE-ya)	LILY, LYDIA
LOIKA	(LOY-ka)	LOIS
LOLEKA	(lo-LEH-ka)	LORETTA
LOLEINA	(lo-LAY-na)	LORRAINE
LUIKA	(lu-WEE-ka)	LOUISA, LOUISE
LUKILA	(lu-KEE-la)	LUCILLE
LUKE	(LOO-ke)	LUCY
LUKIA	(lu-KEE-ya)	LYDIA
MEIPALA	(may-PAH-la)	MABEL
MAKELINA	(MAH-ke-LEE-na)	MADELINE
MAKALEKA	(ma-ka-LEH-ka)	MARGARET

MAKALIKA	*(MAH-ka-LEE-ka)*	MARGUERITE
MALAEA	*(MAH-la-EH-ya)*	MARIA
MALIANA	*(ma-li-YAH-na)*	MARIAN
MELEANA	*(me-le-YAH-na)*	MARIANNE
MALIA	*(ma-LEE-ya)*	MARIE
MELELINA	*(me-le-LEE-na)*	MARILYN
MAKOLI	*(ma-KOH-li)*	MARJORIE
MALINA	*(ma-LEE-na)*	MARLENE
MALEKA	*(ma-LEH-ka)*	MARTHA
MALIA	*(ma-LEE-ya)*	MARY
MEI	*(MAY)*	MAY
MEIPELA	*(may-PEH-la)*	MAYBELLE
MELIKA	*(me-LEE-ka)*	MELISSA
MEKEKE	*(me-KEH-ke)*	MERCEDES
MIKALA	*(mi-KAH-la)*	MICHELLE
MILIKELEKA	*(MEE-li-ke-LEH-ka)*	MILDRED
MILIKENA	*(MEE-li-KEH-na)*	MILLICENT
MILE	*(MEE-le)*	MILLIE
MINEWA	*(mi-NEH-va)*	MINERVA
MINE	*(MEE-ne)*	MINNIE
MILIAMA	*(mi-li-YAH-ma)*	MIRIAM
MONA	*(MOH-na)*	MONA
MIULIELA	*(MEE-yu-li-YEH-la)*	MURIEL
MAILA	*(MEYE-la)*	MYRA
MILENA	*(mi-LEH-na)*	MYRNA
MAKALA	*(ma-KAH-la)*	MYRTLE
NANEKI	*(na-NEH-ki)*	NANCY
NANEKA	*(na-NEH-ka)*	NANETTE
NAKELI	*(na-KEH-li)*	NATALIE
NAOMI	*(NOW-mi)*	NAOMI
NELE	*(NEH-le)*	NELL, NELLIE
NEKI	*(NEH-ki)*	NETTIE
NINA	*(NEE-na)*	NINA
NOLA	*(NOH-la)*	NORA
NOLINA	*(no-LEE-na)*	NOREEN
NOMA	*(NOH-ma)*	NORMA
OLEKA	*(o-LEH-ka)*	OLGA
OLIWA	*(o-LEE-va)*	OLIVE
OLIWIA	*(o-li-VEE-ya)*	OLIVIA
PAMILA	*(pa-MEE-la)*	PAMELA
PAKELEKIA	*(pa-ke-le-KEE-ya)*	PATRICIA
POLEKE	*(po-LEH-ke)*	PAULETTE

POLINA	(po-LEE-na)	PAULINE
MOMI	(MOH-mi)	PEARL
PILIKI	(pi-LEE-ki)	PHYLLIS
PO'IPE	(po-'EE-pe)	PHOEBE
POLE	(POH-le)	POLLY
PELEKILA	(PEH-le-KEE-la)	PRISCILLA
LAHELA	(la-HEH-la)	RACHEL
LEPEKA	(le-PEH-ka)	REBECCA
LOKA	(LOH-ka)	RHODA
LOPEKA	(lo-PEH-ka)	ROBERTA
LOKA	(LOH-ka)	ROSA
LOKALIA	(lo-ka-LEE-ya)	ROSALIE
LOKE	(LOH-ke)	ROSE
LOKELINA	(lo-ke-LEE-na)	ROSELIND
LOKEMELE	(LOH-ke-MEH-le)	ROSEMARY
LUPE	(LOO-pe)	RUBY
LUKA	(LOO-ka)	RUTH
KALE	(KAH-le)	SALLY
KALA	(KAH-la)	SARAH
KOPIA	(ko-PEE-ya)	SOPHIA
KELE	(KEH-le)	SHIRLEY
KEKELA	(ke-KEH-la)	STELLA
KEKEPANIA	(ke-ke-pa-NEE-ya)	STEPHANIE
KUKANA	(ku-KAH-na)	SUSAN
KUKE	(KOO-ke)	SUSIE
KILIWIA	(ki-li-VEE-ya)	SYLVIA
KELEKA	(ke-LEH-ka)	THERESA
KAMA	(KAH-ma)	THELMA
ULUKULA	(OO-lu-KOO-la)	URSULA
WALELIA	(va-le-LEE-ya)	VALERIA
WILA	(VEE-la)	VERA
WELENA	(ve-LEH-na)	VERNA
WALONIKA	(va-LOH-ni-ka)	VERONIKA
WIKOLIA	(vi-ko-LEE-ya)	VICTORIA
WAIOLA	(VEYE-yo-la)	VIOLA
WAIOLEKA	(VEYE-yo-LEH-ka)	VIOLET
WILIKINIA	(vi-li-ki-NEE-ya)	VIRGINIA
WIWIANA	(vi-vi-YAH-na)	VIVIAN
WILEMINA	(wi-le-MEE-na)	WILHELMINA
WILIMA	(wi-li-MAH)	WILMA
WINIPELEKE	(wi-ni-pe-LEH-ke)	WINIFRED
IOLANA	(yo-LAH-na)	YOLANDA
IOWONE	(yo-VOH-ne)	YVONNE

FIND YOUR NAME IN HAWAIIAN, IF KANE*

A'ALONA .... ('a-'a-LOH-na) .... AARON
APELAHAMA ...... (a-PEH-la-HAH-ma) .... ABRAHAM
AKAMU .... (a-KAH-mu) .... ADAM
ALENA........... (a-LEH-na) .... ALAN, ALLEN
ALAPAKI .... (a-la-PAH-ki) .... ALBERT
ALIKA........... (a-LEE-ka) .... ALEX
ALAPAI .... (a-la-PEYE) .... ALFRED
ALEWINA .... (a-le-VEE-na) .... ALVIN
ANALU .... (a-na-LOO) .... ANDREW
AKONI .... (a-KOH-ni) .... ANTHONY
AKE .... (AH-ke) .... ARCHIE, ARCHIBALD
AKA .... (AH-ka) .... ARTHUR
PALEKOLOMAIO... (PAH-le-KOH-lo-MEYE-yo) . BARTHOLOMEW
PAKILE .... (pa-KEE-le) .... BASIL
PENI .... (PEH-ni) .... BEN
PENI'AMINA .... (PEH-ni-ya-MEE-na) ...... BENJAMIN
PELENALAKO ..... (PEH-le-na-LAH-ko) ..... BERNARD
PILA .... (PEE-la) .... BILL
PULUKE .... (pu-LOO-ke) .... BRUCE

* KANE *(KAH-ne)* – Male.

KALAWINA	(ka-la-WEE-na)	CALVIN
KALA	(KAH-la)	CARL
KEKILA	(ke-KEE-la)	CECIL
KALE	(KAH-le)	CHARLES
KILIKIKOPA	(ki-li-ki-KOH-pa)	CHRISTOPHER
KALALENA	(ka-la-LEH-na)	CLARENCE
KALAUKA	(ka-LOW-ka)	CLAUDE
KELEMENEKE	(ke-le-me-NEH-ke)	CLEMENT
KALIPEKONA	(ka-LEE-pe-KOH-na)	CLIFTON
KILILA	(ki-LEE-la)	CYRIL
KANA	(KAH-na)	DAN, DANA
KANIELA	(ka-ni-EH-la)	DANIEL
KAWIKA	(ka-VEE-ka)	DAVID
KENIKA	(ke-NEE-ka)	DENNIS
LIKEKE	(li-KEH-ke)	DICK
KONA	(KOH-na)	DON
KONALA	(ko-NAH-la)	DONALD
KOUKALAKA	(KOW-ka-LAH-ka)	DOUGLAS
KUAIKA	(ku-EYE-ka)	DWIGHT
ELE	(EH-le)	EARL
EKEKA	(e-KEH-ka)	EDGAR
EKEMONA	(e-ke-MOH-na)	EDMOND
EKEWAKA	(e-ke-VAH-ka)	EDWARD
ELUENE	(e-lu-WEH-ne)	EDWIN
ELEMA	(e-LEH-ma)	ELMER
ELELOE	(e-le-LOH-e)	ELROY
ELIKA	(e-LEE-ka)	ERIC
ELENEKI	(e-le-NEH-ki)	ERNEST
IUKINI	(yu-KEE-ni)	EUGENE
PELIKE	(pe-LEE-ke)	FELIX
POLOIKA	(po-LOY-ka)	FLOYD
PALAKIKO	(pa-la-KEE-ko)	FRANCIS
PALANI	(pa-LAH-ni)	FRANK
PELEKE	(pe-LEH-ke)	FREDERICK
KALI	(KAH-li)	GARY
KEOPELE	(KEH-yo-PEH-le)	GEOFFREY
KEOKI	(ke-YOH-ki)	GEORGE
KELALA	(ke-LAH-la)	GERALD
KILIPAKI	(ki-li-PAH-ki)	GILBERT
KOLEKONA	(KOH-le-KOH-na)	GORDON
KELEKOLIO	(ke-le-ko-LEE-yo)	GREGORY
HALOLA	(ha-LOH-la)	HAROLD
HALE	(HAH-le)	HARRY

Hawaiian	Pronunciation	English
HALEWE	(ha-LEH-ve)	HARVEY
HEKEKA	(he-KEH-ka)	HECTOR
HANALE	(ha-na-LEH)	HENRY
HAPAKI	(ha-PAH-ki)	HERBERT
HELEMANO	(he-le-MAH-no)	HERMAN
HAILAMA	(HEYE-la-ma)	HIRAM
HOMELA	(ho-MEH-la)	HOMER
HOLEKA	(ho-LEH-ka)	HORACE
HAOA	(HOW-wa)	HOWARD
HUPEKA	(hu-PEH-ka)	HUBERT
HIU	(HYOO)	HUGH
HUMEPAKA	(hu-me-PAH-ka)	HUMBERT
IWINI	(i-VEE-ni)	IRVING, IRWIN
KEAKA	(ke-AH-ka)	JACK
IAKOPA	(ya-KOH-pa)	JACOB
KIMO	(KEE-mo)	JAMES, JIM
IAKONA	(ya-KOH-na)	JASON
IELOME	(ye-LOH-me)	JEROME
KELE	(KEH-le)	JERRY
IEKE	(ye-KEH)	JESSE
KEO	(KEH-yo)	JOE
IO'ELA	(yo-'EH-la)	JOEL
KEONI	(ke-YOH-ni)	JOHN
IONAKANA	(yo-na-KAH-na)	JONATHON
IOKEPA	(EE-yo-KEH-pa)	JOSEPH
KENEKE	(ke-NEH-ke)	KENNETH
LAULENEKE	(low-le-NEH-ke)	LAWRENCE
LEONE	(le-YOH-ne)	LEO
LEONAKA	(LEH-yo-NAH-ka)	LEONARD
LINEKONA	(LEE-ne-KOH-na)	LINCOLN
LEOPOLO	(LEH-yo-POH-lo)	LEOPOLD
LAIONELA	(LEYE-yo-NEH-la)	LIONEL
LOEKA	(lo-EH-ka)	LLOYD
LOLINA	(lo-LEE-na)	LORRIN
LUI	(LOO-wi)	LOUIS
MALAKOMA	(ma-la-KOH-ma)	MALCOLM
MANUELA	(ma-nu-WEH-la)	MANUEL
MALIONA	(ma-li-YOH-na)	MARION
MALEKO	(ma-LEH-ko)	MARK
MAKINI	(ma-KEE-ni)	MARTIN
MELEWINA	(me-le-VEE-na)	MELVIN
MIKA'ELE	(mi-ka-'EH-le)	MICHAEL, MIKE
NAKANA	(na-KAH-na)	NATHAN

NEKI	(NEH-ki)	NED
NIKOLAO	(ni-ko-LOW)	NICHOLAS
NOMANA	(no-MAH-na)	NORMAN
OLIWA	(o-LEE-va)	OLIVER
OKA	(OH-ka)	OSCAR
OKEWOLEKA	(o-ke-vo-LEH-ka)	OSWALD
OWENE	(o-WEH-ne)	OWEN
PAKELIKA	(pa-ke-LEE-ka)	PATRICK
PAULO	(POW-lo)	PAUL
PELEKI	(pe-LEH-ki)	PERCY
PEKELO	(pe-KEH-lo)	PETER
PILIPO	(pi-LEE-po)	PHILLIP
PELEKEKONA	(pe-le-ke-KOH-na)	PRESTON
LALEPA	(la-LEH-pa)	RALPH
LEI	(LAY)	RAY
LEIMANA	(LAY-MAH-na)	RAYMOND
LEKINALA	(LEH-ki-NAH-la)	REGINALD
LEKE	(LEH-ke)	REX
LIKEKE	(li-KEH-ke)	RICHARD
LOPAKA	(lo-PAH-ka)	ROBERT, BOB
LOPINE	(lo-PEE-ne)	ROBIN
LOKENE	(lo-KEH-ne)	RODNEY
LOKELA	(lo-KEH-la)	ROGER
LOLANA	(lo-LAH-na)	ROLAND
KAMUELA	(ka-mu-WEH-la)	SAMUEL
KIKINE	(ki-ki-NEH)	SIDNEY
KIMONA	(ki-MOH-na)	SIMON
KANALE	(ka-na-LEH)	STANLEY
KIWINI	(ki-WEE-ni)	STEVEN
KEOKOLO	(KEH-yo-KOH-lo)	TED, THEODORE
KOMA	(KOH-ma)	THOMAS, TOM
KIMOKEO	(ki-mo-KEH-yo)	TIMOTHY
WENONA	(we-NOH-na)	VERNON
WIKOLI	(wi-KOH-li)	VICTOR
WINIKENEKE	(wi-ni-ke-NEH-ke)	VINCENT
WILIKILIA	(wi-li-ki-LEE-ya)	VIRGIL
WALAKA	(wa-LAH-ka)	WALTER
WALENA	(wa-LEH-na)	WARREN
WILIPELEKE	(wi-li-pe-LEH-ke)	WILFRED
WENE	(WEH-ne)	WAYNE
WILIKA	(wi-LEE-ka)	WILLARD
WILIAMA	(wi-li-YAH-ma)	WILLIAM
WILE	(WEE-leh)	WILLIE

YOU'LL ALSO MEET UP WITH THESE MEANINGFUL HAWAIIAN NAMES

ANUHEA *(a-nu-HEH-ya)*
Cool, fragrant like a mountain breeze.

'AHULANI *('AH-hu-LAH-ni)*
A heavenly shrine.

'AOLANI *('a-o-LAH-ni)*
Heavenly cloud.

'ALOHI *('a-LOH-hi)*
Shining; brilliant.

AUKAI *(OW-KEYE)*
Seafarer.

'ALOHILANI *('a-LOH-hi-LAH-ni)*
Bright sky.

AULI'I *(ow-LEE-'i)*
Dainty.

ANELA *(a-NEH-la)*
Angel.

EHAKO *(e-HAH-ko)*
Dove.

HALELE'A *(HAH-le-LEH-'a)*
House of Joy.

HAUOLI *(how-OH-li)*
Joy.

HIAPO *(hi-YAH-po)*
First Born.

HIWAHIWA *(HEE-va-HEE-va)*
Precious.

HOKU *(HOH-ku)*
Star.

HOKULANI *(HOH-ku-LAH-ni)*
Stars in the sky.

HO'OMAIKAIANA
(HOH-'o-meye-keye-AH-na)
Blessing.

HO'ONANI *(HOH-'o-NAH-ni)*
To glorify.

HUELANI *(HOO-e-LAH-ni)*
Opening up to heaven.

IAO *(i-YOW)*
Name of a star; cloud supreme.

'IHILANI *('EE-hi-LAH-ni)*
Heavenly splendor.

'INOA PO *('i-NOH-wa POH)*
Dream name.

'IOLANI *('EE-yo-LAH-ni)*
Royal Hawk.

'IPO *('EE-po)*
Darling.

'IWALANI *('EE-wa-LAH-ni)*
The heavenly seabird.

KAHIKAHIWA *(KAH-hi-ka-HEE-va)*
The adorable one.

KAHOKU *(ka-HOH-ku)*
The star.

KAIMANA *(keye-MAH-na)*
Diamond.

KA'IMI *(ka-'EE-mi)*
Seeker.

KAINA *(KEYE-na)*
Cain; little brother.

KAIPO *(KEYE-po)*
The sweetheart.

KA'IULANI *(ka-'EE-u-LAH-ni)*
The highest point in the heaven;
the royal sacred one.

KALANI *(ka-LAH-ni)*
The heavens.

KALEONAHENAHE
(ka-LEH-o-NAH-he-NAH-he)
The soft voice.

KANANI *(ka-NAH-ni)*
The beauty; the pretty one.

KANOA *(ka-NOH-wa)*
The free one.

KANOELANI *(ka-NOH-e-LAH-ni)*
Heavenly mist.

KAOHINANI *(ka-OH-hi-NAH-ni)*
The gatherer of beautiful things.

KAPUA *(ka-POO-wa)*
The blossom.

KAPUNI *(ka-POO-ni)*
The favorite one.

KAU'I *(KOW-'i)*
The beauty.

KAUIKEOLANI
(KOW-wi-KEH-o-LAH-ni)
Placed on heaven's peak.

KA'ULA *(ka-'OO-la)*
A prophet.

KAULANA *(kow-LAH-na)*
Fame.

KAUPILI *(kow-PEE-li)*
Mutual love.

KAWAILALA *(ka-weye-LAH-la)*
Perfume; the fragrance of flowers.

KEAHI *(ke-AH-hi)*
The fire.

KEALOHA *(KEH-ya-LOH-ha)*
The loved one; the beloved.

KEHAULANI *(ke-how-LAH-ni)*
Heavenly dew.

KEKOA *(ke-KOH-wa)*
The courageous one.

KEKUPA'A *(ke-ku-PAH-'a)*
The steadfast one.

KEOLA *(ke-OH-la)*
Life.

KIELE *(ki-'EH-le)*
Fragrant blossom.

KI'ILANI *(KEE-'i-LAH-ni)*
Heavenly image.

KILOHOKU *(KEE-lo-HOH-ku)*
The star gazer.

KINOIKE *(KEE-no-EE-ke)*
The petite one.

KONANE *(ko-NAH-ne)*
Bright as moon light.

KU'ULEI *(KOO-'u-LAY)*
My dear child.

KU'ULEILANI *(KOO-'u-LAY-LAH-ni)*
Heavenly wreath; my royal child.

LA'A *(LAH-'a)*
Sacred; dedicated.

LAELAE *(LAH-e-LAH-e)*
Bright as the shining sun.

LAI *(LEYE)*
Calm.

LAKA *(LAH-ka)*
Attract; tame; goddess of the hula.

LAMA *(LAH-ma)*
Torchlight.

LANA *(LAH-na)*
Buoyant; to float.

LANAKILA *(LAH-na-KEE-la)*
Victorious.

LANI *(LAH-ni)*
Sky; heaven.

LEHUA *(le-HOO-wa)*
A native flower; sacred blossom.

LEI *(LAY)*
Beloved person, child or adult.

LEIALOHA *(LAY-a-LOH-ha)*
Beloved child.

LEILANI *(LAY-LAH-ni)*
Heavenly child.

LEOLANI *(LEH-o-LAH-ni)*
Heavenly voice.

LI'I *(LEE-'i)*
The smallest; often the youngest child in the family is affectionately called Li'i.

LOHELANI *(LOH-he-LAH-ni)*
Hear heaven's bidding.

LOKELANI *(lo-ke-LAH-ni)*
Heavenly rose.

LUANA *(lu-AH-na)*
Enjoyment.

LU'UKIA *(LOO-'u-KEE-ya)*
An ancient chieftess.

MAHEALANI *(ma-HEH-ya-LAH-ni)*
Full moon.

MAHINA *(ma-HEE-na)*
Moon.

MAHOE *(ma-HOH-e)*
Twins.

MAILE *(MEYE-le)*
Myrtle vine.

MAKAMAE *(MAH-ka-MEYE)*
Precious; much desired.

MAKALI'I *(MAH-ka-LEE-'i)*
Tiny; a star constellation, the Pleiades.

MAKANANI *(MAH-ka-NAH-ni)*
Beautiful eyes.

MALUHIA *(MAH-lu-HEE-ya)*
Peace.

MALULANI *(MAH-lu-LAH-ni)*
Under heaven's protection.

MAMO *(MAH-mo)*
Yellow bird.

MANUNUNU *(MAH-nu-NOO-nu)*
Dove.

MAPU *(MAH-pu)*
A rising fragrance.

MAPUANA *(MAH-pu-AH-na)*
Sending forth fragrance.

MELE *(MEH-le)*
A song; poem.

MOANI *(mo-AH-ni)*
Windborn sweetness.

MOANIALA *(mo-AH-ni-AH-la)*
Fresh sweetness brought by the wind.

MOHALA *(mo-HAH-la)*
To unfold and bloom.

NALANI *(na-LAH-ni)*
The heavenly ones (chiefs).

NAMILIMILI *(na-MEE-li-MEE-li)*
The pets or favorites.

NANI *(NAH-ni)*
Beautiful; glory.

NAPUA *(na-POO-wa)*
The flowers.

NOELANI *(no-e-LAH-ni)*
Heavenly mist.

NOHEA *(no-HEH-ya)*
Loveliness.

OKALANI *(OH-ka-LAH-ni)*
Of the heavens.

OLA *(OH-la)*
Life; health.

OLIANA *(OH-li-AH-na)*
Oleander.

OLU *(OH-lu)*
Comfortable; gentle.

ONAONA *(OH-na-OH-na)*
Soft, sweet fragrance.

PA'AO *(pa-'OW)*
The steadfast.

PALILA *(pa-LEE-la)*
A kind of bird.

PIKAKE *(pi-KAH-ke)*
The Hawaiian word for both peacock and jasmine.

PUA'ALA *(POO-wa-'AH-la)*
Fragrant flower.

PUALANI *(POO-wa-LAH-ni)*
Heavenly flower.

PUANANI *(POO-wa-NAH-ni)*
Beautiful flower.

PUKALANI *(POO-ka-LAH-ni)*
Heaven's door.

PUMEHANA *(pu-me-HAH-na)*
Warm.

U'I *(OO-'i)* Beautiful.

U'ILANI *(OO-'i-LAH-ni)*
Gay and restless.

ULUWEHI *(OO-lu-WEH-hi)*
Growing in beauty.

WAINANI *(weye-NAH-ni)*
Beautiful water.

WAIOLI *(weye-OH-li)*
Singing water.

HAWAIIAN IN A FAMILY WAY

ANAKALA .... *(a-na-KAH-la)* .... Uncle

ANAKE .... *(a-na-KEH)* .... Aunt

HOA .... *(HOH-wa)* .... Companion

HOAHANAU .... *(HOH-wa-ha-now)* .... Cousin

HOALAUNA .... *(HOH-wa-LOW-na)* .... Neighbor

HOAPILI .... *(HOH-wa-PEE-li)* .... Intimate friend

KAIKAMAHINE. ...... *(KEYE-ka-ma-HEE-ne)* ...... Daughter

KAIKUA'ANA .... *(keye-KOO-wa-'AH-na)* ...... Brother

KAIKUAHINE .... *(KEYE-ku-wa-HEE-ne)* ...... Sister

KEIKIKANE. .... *(KAY-ki-KAH-ne)* .... Son

KUPUNA .... *(ku-POO-na)* .... Ancestor, Grandparent

KUPUNAKANE .... *(ku-POO-na-KAH-ne)* ..... Grandfather

KUPUNAWAHINE ..... *(ku-POO-na-wa-HEE-ne)* ..... Grandmother

MAHOE .... *(ma-HOH-we)* .... Twin

MAKAHIAPO .... *(MAH-ka-hi-YAH-po)* .... First Born

MAKUA .... *(ma-KOO-wa)* .... Parent

MAKUAHINE. .... *(ma-KOO-wa-HEE-ne)* ...... Mother

MAKUAKANE , , , , , , , . *(ma-KOO-wa-KAH-ne)*. ...... Father

MAMO .... *(MAH-mo)* .... Descendent

MO'OPUNA .... *(MOH-'o-POO-na)* .... Grandchild

'OHANA .... *('o-HAH-na)* .... Relative

PILIALO .... *(PEE-li-AH-lo)* .... Wife

PILIKUA .... *(PEE-li-KOO-wa)* .... Husband

TUTU* .... *(TOO-tu)* .... Granny, Grandmother

*TUTU is not Hawaiian, but is used instead of the actual word, "KUKU" *(KOO-ku)*.

HAWAII'S INVITATIONS, EXPRESSIONS, PHRASES ...

ALOHA

AE *(EYE)*
Yes.

AKAMAI 'OE
(a-ka-meye 'OY)
You're smart.

A 'OLE *('AH- 'OH-le)*
No.

A 'OLE AU E 'IKE
(AH-'OH-le yow 'e 'EE-ke)
I don't know.

AOLE HIKI *(AH-'OH-le HEE-ki)*
No can.

'A 'OLE LOA *('AH 'OH-le LOH-wa)*
Certainly not.

'A 'OLE MAKEMAKE AU
('AH 'OH-le MAH-ke-MAH-ke yow)
I don't wish.

A 'OLE MAOPOPO IA'U
(AH-'OH-le MOW-po-po YAH-'u)
I don't understand.

AOLE PELA *(AH-OH-le PEH-LAH)*
It isn't so.

AOLE PILIKIA
(AH-OH-le pi-li-KEE-ya)
No trouble.

A 'OLE PONO *(AH-'OH-le POH-no)*
It's not right!

AUWE NOHOI E
(ow-WEH no-HOH-'i e)
Boy, oh boy!

AWIWI *(AH-WEE-WEE)*
Be quick!

E *(EH)*
Hey!

HOOMALIMALI

HELE MAI AI *(HEH-le MEYE EYE)*
Come and eat.

HELE MAI; KOMO MAI
(HEH-le MEYE; KOH-mo MEYE)
Come here.

HE MEA IKI *(he MEH-a EE-ki)*
Just a trifle. You're welcome.

HE MEA NUI IA
(he MEH-a NOO-i EE-ya)
An important thing.

HE WAHINE U'I
(HEH wa-HEE-ne OO-'i)
A beautiful woman.

'E AHO IA *('e ah-ho 'EE-ya)*
That's better.

E AI A MA'ANA
(e eye a ma-'AH-na)
Eat to your heart's content.

E HELE KAUA
(e HEH-le ka-'OO-wa)
Let's go.

EI NEI *(AY-NAY)*
You there.

E PAINA *(e pa-'EE-na)*
Dine with us.

HA'I MAI *(HAH-'i MEYE)*
Tell me.

HE AHA KE MEA HOU
(HEH a-ha ke MEH-a HOH)
What's new?

HE KANAKA IKAIKA
(he ka-NAH-ka i-KEYE-ka)
A powerful person.

HELE AKU OE *(HEH-le AH-ku OY)*
Go away; beat it!

HELE *(HEH-le)*
Go! Go ahead!

HONI KAUA WIKIWIKI (kiss me quick)

HIKI *(HEE-ki)*
Okay.

HIKI NO *(hi-ki-NOH)*
Can do.

HO 'I *(HOH-'i)*
Return.

HO'I E MOI *(HOH-'i e MOY)*
Go to bed.

HONI KAUA WIKIWIKI
(HOH-ni ka-OO-wa WEE-ki-WEE-ki)
Kiss me quick.

KOMO MAI. NOU KA HALE!

HO 'OLOHE *(HOH-'o-LOH-he)*
Listen!

HO 'OMALIMALI
(HOH-'o-MAH-li-MAH-li)
Flattery!

HO 'OPAUMANAWA
(HOH-'o POW-ma-NAH-va)
Waste time!

KALA MAI IA'U
(KAH-la meye YAH-'u)
Excuse me.

KALI *(KAH-li)*
Wait!

KALI IKI *(KAH-li EE-ki)*
Wait a little.

KA 'OHI MAI OE *(ka-'OH-hi meye 'OY)*
Hold fast!

KIPA HOU MAI
(KEE-pa HOH MEYE)
Come visit again.

KOKUA MAI *(ko-KOO-a MEYE)*
Help!

KOMO MAI. NOU KA HALE.
(KOH-mo MEYE. NOH ka HAH-le)
Come in. The house is yours.

LAWA *(LAH-WA)*
Enough.

LOKOMAIKA'I OE
(LOH-ko-meye-KAH-'i OY)
You're a good-hearted person.

HAWAII'S WATERS ARE ABUNDANT WITH . . .

Fish you can catch by boat . . .
Fish you can catch from shore . . .
Fish you can spear in the daytime . . .
Fish you can spear at night!
Fish you can eat . . .
Fish you can't eat . . .
Fish you'll thrill to look at . . .
Fish you'll want to look out for . . .
and Shell Fish!

LAMALAMA i'A

AAWA *('a-AH-va)*
A Wrasse Reef Fish, only fair as a food source. Yellow, black and white.
About 4-5 pounds.

AHI *('AH-hi)*
Hawaiian tuna. The Albacore or more often referred to as the Yellow Fin Tuna
is a deep sea fish and a favorite for sashimi (sliced thin, eaten raw with hot
mustard and soy sauce). Sleety blue, under body silvery; fin's yellow. 75-200 lbs.

AHOLEHOLE

AHOLEHOLE
(a-HOH-le-HOH-le)
Big Eye Bass Reef Fish,
meaning "sparkling," it is a
perch-like fish. 6-7 inches.
Bright silver. Excellent for
eating.

AKU *(AH-ku)*
The Hawaiian Aku is an ocean Bonito, a Skipjack. Deliciously edible and
2 to 2½ feet, its coloration is a deep blue with deep blue stripes.

ALA'IHI *(a-la-'EE-hi)*
Squirrel fish that lives in holes in the reef in shallow waters. Usually caught at
night. Said to have been the favorite of King Kamehameha III. 2-2½ inches,
and sometimes 6 inches, 2-4 pounds, up to 7 pounds have been speared.
Bright or rose red. White stripes.

'AMA'AMA *('AH-ma-'AH-ma)*
Mullet fish, greyish in color. Considered a most important fresh water fish by
Hawaiians, being delicious with few bones. Eaten raw or cooked. 8 inches.

A'U *(AH-u)*
Sword fish, Sailfish, Marlin, Spearfish.
Dark grey, almost black. Eaten, but
preferred as a sport fish. 2 to over
13 feet have been caught.

AWEOWEO *('AH-VE-yo-VE-yo)*
Big Eye. Coral fish, 6-8 inches. Red
with white mottling. Good source
of food.

HE'E *(HE-'e)*
Squid, or Octopus as it is widely
referred to, is a favorite island food
found in both reef and offshore waters.
1-4 pounds. Difficult to spear.
Popular as a pupu.

HE'E

HIHIMANU *(hi-hi-MAH-nu)*
Sting Ray. Seldom seen in Hawaiian waters; they do live in outer reefs
and deeper water areas. Gray and spotted, some grow as large as
400 pounds.

HINALEA *(hi-na-LEH-ya)*

Wrasse Fish. Small to moderate-size and brightly colored. 3 to 4 to 10 inches. Eaten raw. A most popular and abundant fish which in ancient times was eaten by women in order to bring on pregnancy.

HUMUHUMUNUKUNUKUAPUAA
(HOO-mu-HOO-mu-NOO-ku-NOO-ku-AH-pu-WAH-a)

Tiny Trigger Fish of various colors. 6-8 inches. Found in deep and shallow waters. Liked by some, considered too bony and smelly by others.

KALA

KIHIKIHI

KAHALA *(ka-HAH-la)*

Amberjack. Deep sea fish. From 30-40 pounds. Sometimes over 100 pounds. 6 feet. Silvery with yellow stripe. A meaty fish. Caught with hook line or speared.

KAKU *(KAH-KOO)*

The Barracuda; its Hawaiian name means "to prod." 4-6 feet. Dark olive-brown and silvery sides, some nearer grey-blue, dark spots. Eaten by certain ones.

KALA *(KAH-la)*

Unicorn Reef Fish. Full grown, 7-8 pounds and 14 to 15 inches. Brownish with a horn.. Edible, but not too tasty.

KAWAKAWA *(KAH-va-KAH-va)*

The Bonito Fish at the adult stage, little tunny, is sometimes called by Hawaiians "pohopoho" (patches) because of some black dots on the belly. Its robust body is generally a cold blue color and 3-4 feet in length. Red fleshed, it is one of the best liked for eating raw or cooked in any way.

KIHIKIHI *(KEE-hi-KEE-hi)*

This Moorish Idol is a Butterfly Reef Fish, 3-6 inches. Color is brilliant, with black and yellow bands. Delicious to some, distasteful to others.

KIKAKAPU *(KEE-KAH-KAH-pu)*

Sacred Fish. A small Butterfly Fish, 3-4 inches. Gaily colored. Not too palatable.

KOLE *(KOH-le)*

Meaning "redness," "raw," "skinned," this reddish-black surgeon tang fish has a yellow ring around its eye and is 4-6 inches. Eaten raw.

KUMU *(KOO-MOO)*

KUMU

Goat Fish. A delicious abundant favorite fish. Red. 5-16 inches. Average speared from 1-3 pounds. Found in deep sea and shallow waters.

LAI *(LEYE)*

Shallow water fish, delicious broiled, dried or baked. 3-16 inches. Silvery, bluish above, whitish underneath.

LAIPALA *(LAH-'EE-PAH-la)*

Surgeon Reef Fish, also called Tang (Kole). Name means "yellow ti-leaf". 3-7 inches. A beautiful bright lemon yellow.

LAUWILIWILINUKUNUKUOIOI *(LOW-WEE-li-WEE-li-NOO-ku-NOO-ku-'OY-'OY)*

Wiliwili leaf. Likened in name to the sharp-beaked Long-Snout Butterfly Fish. Edible but little meat. About 6 inches. Golden yellow with white throat and snout, grey tail.

MAHIMAHI *(MAH-hi-MAH-hi)*

The Dolphin, a little over 5 feet. Sea blue-green with yellow, green and silvery accents. A deep sea fish and a very game fish when caught with a hook. Favorite eating fish among visitors.

MAHIMAHI

MALOLO *(ma-LOH-LOH)*

Flying fish. One foot long. Blue and white. Caught in schools with nets. Swim and skim near surface of deep sea.

MALOLO

MANINI *(ma-NEE-NEE)*

Convict Reef Surgeon Fish. 3-5 inches. Yellow-grey with reddish grey stripes. Considered a delicacy by ancient Hawaiians.

MANO *(ma-NOH)*

Name for Sharks. Sand, Tiger and Hammerheads most common. Largest known, the white shark, rare, not ravenous. Most sharks are 4-8 feet and occasionally larger.

MOANA *(mo-WAH-na)*

A Goat Fish, also call a "Damsel Fish". Speared in reef waters and deep waters also 6-8-12 inches. Most common are red with large scales tipped with yellow. Eaten raw or broiled in ti leaves.

MOI *(MOY)*

Thread Fish, 18 inches to 3 feet. Tawny yellow with light brown stripes. A delicious fish, difficult to spear. Moi means "sovereign".

MU *(MOO)*

Porgie Reef Fish. A silver body with dark bands, red mouth. Average 3-6 pounds. Edible fish.

NAI'A *(NEYE-'ya)*

The friendly, intelligent Porpoise.

MANO

NENUE *(ne-NOO-we)*
Chub Reef Fish. Also called a Rudder or Pilot fish, it varies in
color from silver to dark grey. 4-6 pounds. Some say best when
raw. Either way a popular fish.

NOHU *(NOH-hu)*
Scorpion Reef Fish, which in-
spite of its appearance
is good to eat and
sought for as food. 4-6 pounds.
Basically, reddish-brown.

NUNU *(NOO-NOO)*
Trumpet Fish. 12 inches. A shallow water
fish. Varies in color from grey to pure yellow.

ONO *(OH-no)*
As its name implies, it's delicious. A large mackerel type fish, 5-6 feet long.
Steel blue, with brownish or black stripes, whitish underneath.

MU

OPAKAPAKA *('OH-PAH-ka-PAH-ka)*
There are Blue Snappers and Pink Snappers.
This highly rated sea fish is favored by
visitors. Caught by hook and line over the
off-shore banks. From 12 inches to
2 feet or more.

OPELU *('o-PEH-lu)*
Mackerel Scad. 12 inches.
Plump. Dark blue with white.
Highly prized as food eaten
raw, dried, broiled.

PAKU'IKU'I *(PAH-KOO-'i-KOO-'i)*
A Surgeon Fish about 6-8 inches. Color varies light to dark brown with touches
of orange and blue. Excellent broiled. This Archilles tang is found on shore in
the foam of breaking waves.

PALANI *(pa-LAH-ni)*
Surgeon fish, dark purplish with razor
sharp barbs in the tail. Its strong
odor makes it not very palatable.
6-12 inches.

PAPIOPIO *(PAH-PEE-yo-PEE-yo)*
Generally a dusky color. The young Ulua
is a Reef Fish about 2-2½ feet, which
give the fisherman quite a fight.

LAUWILIWILINUKUNUKUOIOI

PILIKO'A *(PEE-li-KOH-'a)*
Reef fish called a Hawk Fish. 8 inches or less.
Light pink with white bars.
Dusky green head. Not appealing as a food.

MANINI

PUHI *(POO-hi)*

Eels. There are numerous eels in Hawaii. Recorded are the Conger, Snipe, Snake and Moray. Up to 6 feet. Found in shallow waters, 1 foot deep to depths of 150 feet.

UHU *('OO-hu)*

Parrot Fish. A large reef fish. This unique fish is called by this name for its rainbow of colors. Average speared, 8 to 14 pounds. A favorite fish to eat.

UKU *(OO-ku)*

A deep sea Grey Snapper fish, 4-8 pounds and sometimes 30 to 40 pounds. Very tasty. Up to 25 inches, sometimes 3 feet. Difficult to spear.

ULUA *('u-LOO-wa)*

The Jack Crevalle is one of the most popular of game fishes. It frequents shallow and deep depths. Averages 5 feet and 100 to 125 pounds. Color ranges from dark to silvery light.

'U'U *('OO-'OO)*

Menpachi, Squirrel Reef Fish. A delicious tasting fish of the red fish group, 6-8 inches.

WEKE *(VEH-ke)*

Goat Fish, named so because of its yellow barbels. It ranges between 8 to 12 inches. Red and white varieties. Popular fish to eat, it is usually caught with a net rather than speared.

SHELLFISH

'OLEPE *('o-LEH-pe)*
Oyster.

'OPAE *('o-PEYE)*
Shrimp.

OPIHI *('o-PEE-hi)*
Limpet. A highly priced and prized small shellfish caught among the rocks, sometimes at great risk. Favorite at real Hawaiian luaus.

'ULA *('OO-la)*
Hawaiian Lobster, caught in shallow waters of the reef to depths of around 100 feet. Small, averaging 2-4 pounds. Sometimes 7-9 pounds. Delicious!

KNOW THE NAMES OF
HAWAII'S FINE - FEATHERED FRIENDS

HAWAII'S FEATHERED FRIENDS

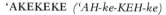

'A *('AH)*

A Red-Footed Booby, this species breeds near the
Kilauea Lighthouse on Kauai and at Ulupau on Oahu.

AE'O *(EYE-'o)*

Referred to as the Hawaiian Stilt, this Black-Necked bird
is found generally in flocks in ponds, marshes and
mudflats on Oahu, Maui, Kauai and Molokai.

'AI LAIKI *('eye-LEYE-ki)*

An all Hawaii resident, this dark-faced ricebird has a plaintive monotone call
reminiscent of the slack-key of Hawaii's own ukulele.

AKIALOA *('a-KEE-ya-LOH-wa)*

Long-curved bill and Creeper-like in its manners,
this bird lives in the rain forest of Kauai.

'AKEKEKE *('AH-ke-KEH-ke)*

This Ruddy Turnstone is found throughout the
islands on beaches, mudflats, pastures and ploughed fields.

'AKEPA *('a-KEH-pa)*

Kauai and the Big Island of Hawaii are the homes of
this very little creeper-like bird.

'AKIAPOLA AU *('a-KEE-ya-po-la 'OW)*

A bird with a very unusual bill, this rare bird lives on the Big Island in the
forests and in and around the Volcano National Park.

'AKOHEKOHE *('a-KOH-he-KOH-he)*

A crested Honeycreeper, it is the rarest of living Native
Hawaiian mountain birds and lives only on the island of Maui.

'ALAE KE'OKE'O *('a-LEYE KEH-'o-KEH-'o)*

This American Coot bird is particularly abundant at Kanaha
Pond on Maui, because of the suitable ponds or swamps.

'ALAE 'ULA *('a-LEYE 'OO-la)*

The Gallinule, a shy, retiring bird, is found on Kauai, Molokai and Oahu.

'ALALA *('a-LAH-la)*

This rare bird is endemic to the island of Hawaii only.
Also referred to as the Hawaiian Crow in the Kona area.

'AMAKIHI *('a-ma-KEE-hi)*

Similar to a Creeper, this singer with a trilling song-like
tweet is found on all forest areas on all Islands.

'ANIANIAU *('a-ni-ya-ni-YOW)*

The smallest of the Loxop species, this bright
yellowish-green bird is found in the forested areas of Kauai.

'EWA 'EWA

'A'O *('AH-'o)*

Now and then, you'll spot this bird, known as Newell's Shearwater, near Pokai Bay on Oahu. Most of the time he lives on Kauai.

'APAPANE *('a-pa-PAH-ne)*

This crimson colored beauty is seen throughout the Islands and in keeping with Hawaii's reputation it has a repertoire of many pleasing songs.

'EHAKO *('EH-ha-KOH)*

This Spotted Dove is found on all the Hawaiian Islands in open country.

'ELEPAIO *('e-le-PEYE-yo)*

This island species inhabits forested areas and also can be seen on trails on Oahu, at Kokee, Kauai and in the Volcanic National Park on Hawaii.

'ELEPAIO

'EWA 'EWA *('EH-va 'EH-va)*

This Sooty Tern bird breeds off Oahu on the islands of Moku Manu and Manana (Rabbit Island). Though it prefers sandy flats, it does nest on rocky ledges.

HUNAKAI *(hu-na-KEYE)*

The Sanderling spends its winters in Hawaii taking in all the islands at its pleasure.

'I'IWI *('i-'EE-vi)*

On the islands of Oahu, Hawaii, Kauai and Maui, lives this rarely seen and once believed extinct, bright vermilion

'i 'IWI

bird whose precious 'I'iwi feathers were used years ago, in featherwork by the Hawaiians.

'I'O *('EE-yo)*

Hawaiian Hawk seen on the Big Island of Hawaii only, on the mountain slopes of Mauna Kea and Mauna Loa, and sometimes in the Volcanic National Park and near Hilo.

'IWA *('EE-va)*

The Great Frigatebird, who resides on Moku Manu.

KIOEA *(ki-yo-WEH-ya)*

A frequent visitor, this Bristle-Thighed Curlew has been seen on Oahu at Kaneohe Bay, Kuapa Pond and on sandy beaches, along the windward side of the island.

KOAE KEA *(ko-WAH-'e KEH-ya)*

A white-tailed Tropicbird, he is also a beautiful sight in flight and found on all main Hawaiian Islands.

KOAE ULA *(ko-WAH-'e 'OO-la)*

A Red-Tailed Tropicbird, he is spectacular in flight, performing with the grace of a ballet dancer. He's been observed off the Windward coast of Oahu from Koko Head to Mokoli'i.

'IO

KOLEA *(ko-LEH-ya)*

You'll recognize this bird as the American Golden Plover found on all the islands on mudflats, lawns, fields and grassy mountain slopes.

KOLOA MAOLI *(ko-LOH-wa MOW-li)*

Suggestive of the Mallard, this Hawaiian Duck resides on Kauai.

KOLOA MAPU *(ko-LOH-wa MAH-pu)*

This Pintail Duck is found on all the Hawaiian Islands where there are fresh or brackish ponds.

MANU KAPALULU *(MAH-nu KAH-pa-LOO-lu)*

This California Quail import is common on Hawaii, Molokai and Maui.

MANU LI'ILI'I *(MAH-nu LEE-'i-LEE-'i)*

An all Hawaiian Islands inhabitant, this chirpy, twittering House Sparrow is considered a noisy nuisance, but to the visitors especially, his common and audacious presence, appeals.

MAUI PARROTBILL *(MOW-wi)*

This rare species, with the most enormous bill for its size lives on the Island of Maui in the upper forest on the slopes of Haleakala.

NENE *(NEH-ne)*

The Nene, Hawaii State Bird, or rather goose, is being propagated on the Islands of Hawaii and Maui where it lives high on mountain slopes and lava flows.

NOIO *(NOY-yo)*

Seen at Kaneohe Bay, on the ponds of the Marine Corps Air-Station, the off-shore islands, especially Moku Manu, this White Capped Noddy is also referred to as the Hawaiian Noddy.

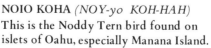

NOIO KOHA *(NOY-yo KOH-HAH)*

This is the Noddy Tern bird found on islets of Oahu, especially Manana Island.

NUKUPU'U *(nu-ku-POO-'u)*

This very rare bird, lives in the upper forests of Kauai and is known by its short trill type song that comes out as "Kee-wit".

'OMA'O *('o-MAH-'o)*

The 'Oma'o is seen on Kauai in the Alakai Swamp area, in the Volcanic National Park on Molokai and forest areas along the Saddle Road on the Big Isle.

'O'O'A'A *('OH-'OH-'AH-'AH)*

This active rare bird is always on the move. He is known as the Kauai 'O'O, for he has only been seen in the forest of Kauai's Alakai Swamps.

PIHA'E KELO
(MYNAH)

'O'U *('OH-'OO)*

A Big Island resident, rarely seen, the 'O'u rates as a great island songster.

PAKALAKALA *(pa-KAH-la-KAH-la)*

A small colony of this bird, the Gray-Backed Tern is found on the eastern slope of Moku Manu.

PALILA *(pa-LEE-la)*

Strictly a Big Island of Hawaii resident, this attractive bird is known as the "Mamane Eater".

PIHA'E KELO *(PEE-ha-'e KEH-lo)*

Hawaii's well-known Mynah is a most intelligent and entertaining critter, living throughout the islands. Considered a nuisance by some, amusing by others, he also shares a rare spot as a pet who can be taught to talk, to say "Mahalo Nui Loa," "Aloha," and a few other phrases, best not mentioned.

PUAIOHI *(pu-weye-YOH-hi)*

Extremely rare, this bird has been seen only in the Alakai Swamp forest area on the island of Kauai. Also known as Small Kauai Thrush and Palmer's Thrush.

PUAIOHI

PUEO *(pu-WEH-yo)*

Common on Kauai and Haleakala, Maui, this Short-Eared Owl is prominent in Hawaiian mythology.

'UA'U KANI *('u-WAH-'u KAH-ni)*

A graceful bird that soars low over the water when in flight, this Wedge-Tailed Shearwater is found off the Island of Oahu, on Manana, Popoia, Moku Manu and on Kauai close to the Kilauea Lighthouse.

'U A'U *('u-WAH-'u)*

His English moniker, is the "Dark-Rumped Petrel". Said to sound like a yapping dog, this unique bird lives on Maui and Hawaii, breeding in Maui's Haleakala and in volcanic slopes on the Big Isle.

ULILI

'ULILI *('u-LEE-li)*

Mostly a winter visitor to the islands, this Wandering Tattler is found along rocky coasts and on mudflats.

ANIMALS, INSECTS, REPTILES, FOWLS ...
HAWAII HAS 'EM, TOO!

ALAE *(a-LEYE)* . . . . Mud Hen
'ANEKELOPA *('a-NEH-ke-LOH-pa)* . . . . . . Antelope
EKAKE *(e-KAH-ke)* . . . . Donkey
ELELU *(e-le-LOO)* . . . . Cockroach
HIPA *(HEE-pa)* . . . . Sheep
HONU *(HOH-nu)* . . . . Turtle
I'A *(EE-'a)* . . . . Fish
IOLE *(i-YOH-le)* . . . . Mouse, Rat
IOLE LAPAKI *(i-YOH-le la-PAH-ki)* . . . . . Rabbit
ILIO *(i-LEE-yo)* . . . . Dog
ILIO HOLO I KAUAUA
(i-LEE-yo HOH-lo EE KOW-oo-wa-OO-wa) . Monk Seal

I'A

PUA'A

KA KA *(KAH KAH)* . . . . Domestic Duck
KAO *(KOW)* . . . . Goat
KEA *(KEH-ya)* . . . . Boar
KIA *(KEE-ya)* . . . . Deer
KOLOA *(ko-LOH-wa)* . . . . Wild Duck
LIO *(LEE-yo)* . . . . Horse
MANAKUKE *(MAH-na-KOO-ke)* . . . . Mongoose
MOA *(MOH-wa)* . . . . Chicken
MO'O *(MOH-'o)* . . . . Lizard, Gecko
NAI'A *(NEYE-'a)* . . . . Porpoise
NALO *(NAH-lo)* . . . . Fly
NALOMELI *(NAH-lo-MEH-li)* . . . . Honey Bee

ILIO

POPOK

NAONAO LELE *(NOW-NOW LEH-le)* .... Termite
NAONAO *(NOW-NOW)* .... Ant
'OPE'APE'A *('o-PEH 'AH-pe-AH)* .... Bat
PELEHU *(PEH-le-HOO)* .... Turkey
PIKAKE *(pi-KAH-ke)* .... Peacock
PIPI *(PEE-pi)* .... Cattle, Beef
PIPIKANE *(PEE-pi-KAH-ne)* .... Bull
PIPIWAHINE *(PEE-pi-wa-HEE-ne)* ...... Cow
POLOKA *(po-lo-KAH)* .... Frog
POPOKI *(po-POH-ki)* .... Cat
PUA'A *(pu-WAH-'a)* .... Pig
PUEO *(pu-WEH-yo)* .... Owl
'UHINI *('u-HEE-ni)* .... Grasshopper

MO'O

PUEO

HAWAII'S HANAI*
GREETINGS - SALUTATIONS
TOASTS

MAHALO

ARIGATO *(a-ri-GAH-toh)*
"Thank You" in Japanese.

BANZAI *(BAHN-ZEYE)*
A cheer in Japanese meaning, "Ten thousand years of life."

ICHIBAN *(EE-chi-BAHN)*
"Number One" in Japanese.

KON NICHI WA *(KOHN NEE-chi WAH)*
"Good Day" in Japanese.

KUMOSTA *(ku-mos-TAH)*
"Hello" or "How do you do" in Ilocano and Tagalog.

KUN HEE FAT CHOY *(kun HEE faht CHOY)*
(Cantonese) Chinese for "Happy New Year".

KUNG HEE FAT CHOY

SAYONARA

KUNG HO SING DAN *(kun HOH sin DAHN)*
(Cantonese) Chinese for "Merry Christmas".

MABUHAY *(ma-BOO-heye)*
Filipino expression for "Long live . . . joy".

MALIGA YANG PASKO *(MAH-li-ga yang PAHS-ko)*
"Merry Christmas" in Tagalog.

MERI KURISUMASU *(me-REE ku-REE-su-MAH-su)*
"Merry Christmas" in Japanese.

NAIMBAG A PASKUA YO *(na-IM-BAHG a pas-KWA yo)*
"Merry Christmas" in Ilocano (a Filipino dialect).

OHAYO *(o-HEYE-yo)*
"Good morning" in Japanese.

SAYONARA *(sa-yo-NAH-ra)*
"Good-bye" in Japanese.

SUNG TAN CHUKA HAMNIDA
(sun tan CHOO-ka ham-NEE-da))
"Merry Christmas" in Korean.

MABUHAY

*HANAI *(ha-NEYE)* — Adopt.

TOASTS: ("Here's to your health"; "Bottoms up!"; "Drink up!"; etc.)

A VOTRE SANTE *(a VOT-tra SANT)*	French
CHEERIO	English
GUN PAE *(gun PEYE)*	Korean
HERE'S HOW	American
HERE'S TAE YE *(here's TEYE ye)*	Scottish
IS YGIAN *(ISH i-GEE-an)*	Greek
KAN PAI *(kan PEYE)*	Japanese
KHON PUI *(kon POO-i)*	Chinese
LA VASCHE ZDOROVYE *(la vash ZDROV-ye)*	Russian
L'CHAYIM *(la-HIM)*	Jewish
MALIGAYANG BATI *(ma-li-ga-yang BAH-ti)*	Filipino
MANULA *(ma-NOO-la)*	Tahitian
NA ZDROWIE *(na ZDROV-ve)*	Polish
OKOLE MALUNA *(o-KOH-le ma-LOO-na)*	Hawaiian
PROSIT *(PROH-sit)*	German
SALUD *(sa-LOOD)*	Spanish, Mexican
SALUDE *(sa-LOOD)*	Portuguese
SALUTE *(sa-LOO-te)*	Italian
SKOAL *(SKOHL)*	Scandinavian

KAMAU!

*KAMAU! *(ka-MOW)* . . . . A toast!

HAWAII'S HANAI*
FASHION WEAR

FILIPINO

BARONG TAGALOG *(ba-RONG ta-GAH-log)*
The cool embroidered shirt of the Filipino male.

HAPI COAT *(HAH-pi)*
A short garment with straight sleeves, similar to the Kimono.

JAPANESE

KIMONO *(ki-MOH-no)*
The traditional garment of the Japanese.

LAVA LAVA *(LAH-va LAH-va)*
A Samoan garment, similar to the Hawaiian malo. Worn by men.

OBI *(OH-bi)*
The sash or belt worn with the Japanese Kimono is called Obi. The material is often exquisitely embroidered, and is highly prized.

*HANAI *(ha-NEYE)* – Adopt.

CHINESE

KOREAN

TABI *(TAH-bi)*
A Japanese socklike foot covering which has a division between the large toe and the other toes.

TERNO *(TER-no)*
A long gown with wing-like sleeves worn by Filipino women.

ZORI *(ZOH-ri)*
These low Japanese thong slippers, also called "go-aheads" or "grass-slippers", are worn by men, women and children in Hawaii.

PEDICAB

CHOPSTICKS

SHOJI

ZABUTON

TINIKLING

AIKIDO *(eye-KEE-do)*
One form of Japanese self-defense.

ARIRANG *(AH-ri-RANG)*
A haunting Korean folk song
describing the sadness of two
lovers parting.

BAYAW *(ba-YOW)*
English-Filipino Ilocano meaning
for "Filipino Style" with the men
in one group and the women
in another.

BON DANCE *(pronounced as appears)*
A Japanese-English term for a
Japanese folk dance performed
in mid-July in Hawaii as a part
of the o-bon "festival of the dead".

*HANAI *(ha-NEYE)* — Adopt.

CHAWAN CUT *(cha-WAN)*
Japanese and English term for the "rice-bowl" style of haircut that looks as if a bowl had been placed on the head, and the hair trimmed around its edges.

CHOPSTICKS *(pronounced as appears)*
Utensils for eating oriental foods.

DORAJI *(do-RAH-ji)*
Korean expression for "bell flower".

FALE *(FAH-le)*
Samoan equivalent for Hawaiian "Hale" or house.

HANAMICHI *(HAH-na-MEE-chi)*
Extension of the Japanese stage in drama.

KABUKI *(ka-BOO-ki)*
The traditional popular Japanese drama.

KARATE *(KAH-ra-TEH)*
Japanese martial art.

KOTO *(KOH-toh)*
Musical instrument of Japan introduced into Hawaii.

MAMA-SAN *(pronounced as appears)*
Japanese-English. Means: "Good, worthy, Mother." A term of high respect for an older woman of Japanese ancestry.

NAICHI JIN *(NEYE-chi JIN)*
Refers to people from Japan (Naichi meaning "inner land").

NISEI *(NEE-say)*
Literally means "second generation" away from Japan, but it has acquired the meaning "first generation" born in Hawaii.

ORIGAMI *(OH-ri-GAH-mi)*
The Japanese art of paper-folding.

PAPA-SAN *(pronounced as appears)*
Japanese-English. Means "Good, worthy Father."

PEDICAB
(pronounced as appears)
A bicycle-drawn, Chinese-style cab.

RICKSHAW *(pronounced as appears)*
A hand-pulled Chinese cab.

SANSEI *(SAN-SAY)*
Third generation away from Japan and second generation born on the islands.

SHAMISEN *(SHA-mi-SEN)*
Musical instrument of Japanese origin introduced into Hawaii.

SHIBAI *(shi-BEYE)*
A Japanese term which has come to mean, in political circles in Hawaii, "making a dramatic production to obscure a point."

SHIBUI *(shi-BOO-yi)*
In designing of clothing, the Japanese term for elegance without undue ornamentation.

SHOJI *(SHO-ji)*
Japanese-English. Sliding door made of lightweight wood, usually covered with rice paper.

SUMO *(SOO-moh)*
Japanese sport of wrestling.

TOKONOMA *(TOH-ko-NOH-ma)*
A Japanese term for displaying an object of art or flower arrangement.

TINIKLING *(ti-NIK-ling)*
Native Filipino bamboo dance.

TSUNAMI *(tsu-NAH-mi)*
Commonly a "tidal wave", though in Japanese it means "ocean wave".

ZABUTON *(zah-bu-TON)*
The Japanese term for the large floor cushions now found in homes of people of all ethnic groups in the islands.

ABURAGE *(AH-bu-ra-GAY)*
Japanese word for thin, oblong pieces
of "tofu" fried in deep fat.

ADOBO *(a-DOH-bo)*
A Filipino word describing a dish of
pork, garlic and chicken.

AEMONO *(EYE-mo-no)*
Japanese word describing fresh fish or
shellfish mixed with vegetables and
served raw or boiled, and then mixed
with "sesame," "miso," or "tofu" and
vinegar, "shoyu," salt and sugar.

AJINOMOTO *(a-JEE-no-MOH-to)*
Japanese word for monosodium glutamate.

BAGOONG *(ba-GOONG)*
A hot paste-like sauce which is as powerful
as its name suggests.

BAKALAW *(ba-ka-LOW)*
A Filipino codfish stew.

CHINESE

HAWAII'S
HANAI
KAUKAU

BOK CHERK HAR *(BAK cherk HAH)*
A Chinese way of boiling shrimp with a
dipping sauce.

BOK CHIT GAI *(BAK chit GEYE)*
Chinese for coddled chicken.

CARNE EN SALSA ROJA
(KAR-nee en SAL-sah ROH-hah)
Beef in red chili sauce, a Mexican favorite.

CARNE EN SALSA VERDE
(KAR-nee en SAL-sah VAYR-day)
Beef in green tomato sauce.

CHAR SIU *(CHAR SYU)*
Chinese sweet roast pork.

CHAWANMUSHI *(CHA-wang-MOO-shi)*
Japanese description of hot dish of egg
or meat custard steamed in a small bowl.

CHORIZO *(cho-REE-zo)*
A Portuguese sausage.

CHOW FUN *(chow-FUN)*
Chinese dish of wide noodles cooked with por

JAPANESE

CHUK *(TCHOOK)*
Chinese rice soup.

CHUN *(pronounced as appears)*
Meat or fish cut into small pieces and rolled in flour before being fried.

CHUTNEY *(CHUT-NEE)*
A jam-like condiment made with fruits, raisins, dates, onions, spices and vinegar.

CURRY *(KER-REE)*
A condiment powder consisting of ground spices.

DAIKON *(deye-KON)*
A giant Japanese turnip-sized radish, often pickled.

DOMBURI *(DOM-bu-REE)*
Japanese word for large bowl. You'll come across this word on all Japanese menus.

GAR DOO GAI *(gar-DOO-gai)*
Chinese prepared chicken.

HIBACHI *(hi-BAH-chi)*
A Japanese charcoal brazier; a portable stove.

HULIHULI CHICKEN *(HOO-li-HOO-li)*
A Hawaiian-Haole version for chicken roasted on a spit or rotisserie. Huli means — "to turn".

KAKI MOCHI *(KAH-ki MOH-chi)*
Japanese rice crackers usually eaten while sipping tea or at snack time.

KAMABOKO *(KAH-ma-BOH-koh)*
Japanese boiled fish paste, in Hawaii considered as fish cake.

KANTEN *(kan-TENG)*
A Japanese vegetable gelatin derived from seaweed, sold in blocks. Melted with fruit and flavoring added, it is served as a dessert. Kanten is the chief ingredient in many Japanese confections.

KIM CHEE *(kim CHEE)*
Korean highly spiced and aromatic pickled vegetables. Principle ingredient is Won Bok cabbage, highly seasoned with red pepper, garlic, onion and soy-bean.

KIYURI NAMASU *(ki-YOO-ri na-ma-SOO)*
Japanese dish of cucumbers prepared in a sweet and sour way and served as a salad or relish.

KUN KOKI *(KUN ko-KEE)*
Korean barbecued meat cooked with toasted "sesame seeds", garlic, green onions, hot pepper and with "shoyu" and "sesame" oil.

LI HING MUI *(LEE hing MOO-yi)*
Chinese salty plums.

LINGUICA *(ling-GWEE-sa)*
A spicy hot Portuguese sausage.

LOCOMOCO *(LOH-ko-MOH-ko)*
A simple Japanese-Haole dish that is a "quickie" combination of rice, hamburger and fried eggs served in a "saimin" bowl and seasoned with soy sauce. Hawaii's local version of "steak 'n eggs."

LYCHEE *(leye-CHEE)*
A Chinese nut that tastes like a grape. To eat, you remove the thin hard shell on the outside. The fruit is like a peeled grape.

MALASADAS *(MAH-la-SAH-daz)*
Popular Portuguese doughnuts with no holes. Outside sprinkled with sugar. Eaten hot. Mmmmmmm.

MANAPUA *(MAH-na-POO-wa)*
A Chinese steamed dumpling type of bun stuffed with pork, pot roast, chicken or such, then steamed.

MANDU *(MAHN-DOO)*
Very small meat pie, steamed and filled with meat, bean curd, bean sprouts, vegetables and Kim Chee, all chopped together. A Korean dish.

MANJU *(man-JOO)*
Japanese word for little steamed buns with sweet gelatine bean-paste in the center.

MESHIMONO *(MEH-shi-MOH-noh)*
Japanese description for fish, meat or vegetables boiled with rice. Also, fish meat or vegetables poured over rice. Both are served in a "domburi".

MIRIN *(MEE-RING)*
A sweet wine used to flavor boiled food. It is made from steamed glutinous rice in which a malt-mold is cultured, and then mixed with strong "sake".

MISO *(MEE-so)*
A Japanese mixture of salt, malt and mashed soy beans with its liquor put in a large tub and allowed to ferment. Used for "miso-soup" and for flavoring.

MISO SOUP *(MEE-so)*
A delicious, nutritious Japanese soup made with white soy bean curd, "miso".

MOCHI *(mo-CHEE)*
A Japanese preparation of a glutinous rice, steamed, mashed in a mortar, and made into various shapes, usually flat, round cakes ¼ inch thick, 1½ by 2 inches. Used in the New Year "Zoni" ("Miso or clear soup with "Mochi").

NAM YUE *(nam YOO-e)*
Chinese bean curd.

NORI *(NOH-ri)*
Japanese word for "seaweed".

PANSIT *(pan-SIT)*
A Filipino noodle dish of distinction.

PAO DOCE *(pon DOOS)*
An island favorite. Portuguese bread. This is a sweet egg-rich round loaf of bread with a golden crustiness. Best broken, then sliced. Warmed and buttered, it is really out of this world!

PIPI BELLPEPPER *(PEE-pi)*
A Chinese-Haole dish prepared with thin slices of beef (pipi) sauteed in a special soy sauce mixture, combined with chopped bellpeppers and a hint of sesame oil.

PORK TOFU *(toh-FOO)*
A Haole-Japanese dish consisting of pork, onions and other vegetables with hunks of tofu, bean curd.

PUPU *(POO-pu)*
An Hawaiian-Haole version of an hors d' oeurvre or appetizer consisting of small sausages or miniature hot dogs, shrimp, meat sticks, sushi, etc.

RUMAKI *(ROO-ma-ki)*
A Japanese "pupu" consisting of chicken livers and water chestnuts wrapped in bacon and broiled.

SAIMIN *(SEYE-min)*
Japanese noodles cooked in a broth of chicken, pork or fish.

SAKANA *(sa-ka-NAH)*
Japanese fish prepared in a variety of ways.

SAKE *(SAH-ke)*
Japanese wine made from white rice and malt-mould and water. Served hot; it is also used to flavor soups or boiled foods.

SASHIMI *(sa-shi-MEE)*
A Japanese "pupu" (hors d'oeurve) favorite. You dip it in a sauce of shoyu, seasoned with ginger, horseradish or hot mustard.

SEE MUI *(SEE MOO-wi)*
Chinese sour and salty plums; a treat that Hawaii's keiki love like candy!

SENBEI *(sem-BAY)*
A Japanese wafer-like cookie.

SHINRAN TOFU *(shin-ran toh-FOO)*
A Chinese dessert using Mandarin orange slices, Lichee, cherries, peach slices, and a special gelatin consisting of almond extract and milk.

SHOYU *(sho-YOO)*
A liquid made from roasted corn and steamed soy beans mixed with malt-mould and fermented. Also spelled "Soya" (Chinese style). Universally known as Soy Sauce. Used in all Oriental cooking.

SINIGANG *(si-ni-GANG)*
A Filipino soup delicacy of meat or
fish and tomatoes, cooked in water
with tamarind, guavas or green
mangoes added for tart flavor.

SOMEN *(SOH-MEN)*
A packaged Japanese vermicelli.

SUIMONO *(SOO-i-MOH-no)*
A clear Japanese soup flavored with
seasonings and with fish or meat or
vegetables added.

FILIPINO

SUKIYAKI *(su-ki-YAH-ki)*
The most popular of the Japanese
saucepan dishes served at the table.
Consists of beef, pork or chicken with
vegetables and noodles. Diner has a choice
of eating it with a raw egg dropped on top and cooked from heat of ingredients.
Uncooked ingredients are placed in cooker before them and picked out with
chopsticks by diner. Delicious!

SUNOMONO *(SOO-no-MOH-no)*
A Japanese dish of vegetables, fish or shellfish used either raw or boiled quickly
and flavored with vinegar.

SURIBACHI *(SOO-ri-BAH-chi)*
A Japanese earthenware mortar with a wooden pestle used for crushing or
grinding sesame seeds and "miso", etc., into a paste.

SUSHI *(su-SHEE)*
A Japanese favorite as popular in the islands as the American hot dog.
Slightly vinegar-falvored, rolled rice is filled with vegetables, fish, egg-strips
and wrapped in seaweed or fried egg-skin.

TAKO *(TAH-ko)*
Japanese word for octopus.

TAMARIND *(TAM-a-RIND)*
The tart, brown fruit from the Tamarind tree which sometimes provides
the characteristic sour taste in Filipino dishes.

TEMPURA *(tem-pu-RAH)*
Japanese method of cooking fish or vegetables dipped in batter and fried in
deep fat.

TERIBURGER *(TEH-ri BUR-GER)*
A Japanese-Haole preparation using the hamburger cooked with a teriyaki
sauce.

TERIYAKI SAUCE *(TEH-ri-YAH-ki)*
Japanese sauce made with shoyu (soy sauce), ginger, sugar and other seasonings of choice.

TERIYAKI STEAK *(TEH-ri-YAH-ki)*
A Japanese-Haole treatment of steak which is marinated in teriyaki sauce.

TINOLA *(ti-NOH-la)*
A Filipino chicken soup often made with the addition of garlic, ginger and green papaya cubes.

TOFU *(TOH-FOO)*
Japanese name for soy bean curd. A curd made of the liquid from soy beans, softened in water and crushed, boiled and solidified by magnesium chloride.

TSUKEMONO *(TSU-ke-MOH-noh)*
Japanese radishes, turnips or greens pickled in rice bran and salt, or only salt.

TSUKUDANI *(TSU-ku-DAH-ni)*
Small fish, shellfish or seaweed boiled down in shoyu, salt and sugar, and made into preserved food.

UDON *(u-DONG)*
Japanese noodles. A kind of vermicelli like "soba," but made of corn flour.

WIKIWIKI BURGER *(WEE-ki-WEE-ki)*
A Hawaiian-Haole term for a hamburger put together in a "wikiwiki" (fast, hurried) manner. Usually served with a pineapple slice.

WON BOK *(WAHN BAHK)*
A tall, slender Chinese cabbage.

WUN TUN *(WON TON)*
Chinese meat dumplings, fried in deep fat until crisp, served on menus and as a "pupu."

WUN TUN MEIN *(WON TON MIN)*
Wun Tun served in a soup.

YAKITORI *(YAH-ki-TOH-ri)*
Japanese styled marinated chicken, threaded on bamboo skewers with livers and onions, broiled, then dipped in sesame seeds.

YOKAN *(yo-KAHN)*
Japanese confection made with red bean paste and gelatin and molded in oblong slabs.

KOREAN

HAWAII'S PIDGIN EXPRESSIONS

AH, MINAH . . . . Of no importance; no worry; a minor thing.

ALLA SAME . . . . All the same.

ALREADY . . . . Yet.

'ASS AWRI . . . . That's alright.

'ASS OK . . . . That's OK.

'ASSWHYHARD! . . . . That's why it's hard. Too bad.

BLALA . . . . Like Bla, it means brother.

BROKE MY MOUTH . . . . The food tastes so good.

BUS YOU UP . . . . I'll beat you up.

BUMBYE . . . . In the future; by and by, soon.

CALABASH COUSINS . . . Not blood relations but very close friends.

CAN DO . . . . Can; able to do.

CATCH . . . . Get.

COAST HAOLE . . . . Caucasion from the West Coast or any person newly arrived from any part of the mainland.

Calabash Cousins

COOL HEAD MAIN TING..	Keep calm; keep a level head; don't panic.
DA KINE	Synonymous with "thingamajig," "whatdeyacalit," "so and so," or "whosis." Whatever the speaker chooses it to mean.
DA BUGGAH HANA PA'A	Stuck.
EH, BRAH!............	Hey, you!

GO FOR BROKE

FADDA	Father.
FOGET IT	Forget it.
GEEV UM	Give them everything; give them the works.
GO FOR BROKE	Make the extreme effort; go all out.
GUD KINE DIS	This is very good.
HANA WAI DA YARD....	Water the yard.
HE BEEN GO	He went.
HE STAY GO	He is going.
HELE ON!	Come on!
HEY, BOOL!	Hey, you!
HEY, BRUDDAH, HEY, BLA!	Hey, brother!
HOWZIT?	How are you?

HUMBUG	Bothersome; nuisance.
I SCARE!	I'm afraid.
I SHAME	I'm embarrassed.
JUNKS	Small personal things.
KONA WEATHER	Muggy weather
NO CAN	Cannot.
NO HUHU	Don't be angry.
NO MAKE LIKE DAT	Don't do that.
NO MAKE MENTION ...	Don't mention it.
MADDA	Mother.
MANINI LOOKING	Skimpy looking; inadequate.
MOAH BETTA!	More Better!
NO BIG TING	It doesn't matter.
NO BUG, MOAH BETTA YOU FOGET IT.......	Don't plague. Better to forget such a thing.

HUMBUG

PUBLIC TELEPHONE

NO PAU ALREADY . . . . . Not finished yet.

NO PILIKIA . . . . It's no trouble. No difficulty.

NO-STOP . . . . Is not here.

NUMBAH ONE . . . . The best.

NUMBAH ONE LUNA . . . . . Head man. The one in charge.

ON THE KINIPOPO . . . . . . Right on the ball.

ONE-FINGER POI . . . . One finger method for scooping up poi when it is thick.

ONO LOOKING . . . . Delicious; delectable.

OPEN YOUR MAKA . . . . . .Watch what you're doing.

PILAU BUGGAH	You no-good person!
PAU HANA TIME	Quitting time.
PIO THE LIGHT	Turn out the light.
PIPI STEW	Beef stew.
POI DOG	A strain of dog used for hunting wild pigs and formerly fed on poi. Also, a mongrel.
SAVVY	Know; know how to.
SHAKA	Right on, brother. That's great.
STOP	Is here.
SUCK 'EM UP!	Drink up!
SUCK WIND!	Go hungry. Lose out.
SUM GUD TING!	Something good, swell.
TAKE OFF	Go like the wind.
TALK STORY	Tell stories; conversation or discussion.
TWO-FINGER POI	Poi of a thinner consistency.
US GO	Let's go.
WASTE TIME	No sense to that; distasteful; useless thing; boring.
WHACK 'EM!	Eat them up! Finish them up!
WHERE YOU WEN' GO? ...	Where did you go?
WHOSE ONE DIS?	Whose is this?
YOU WIPE OUT!	You've had it!

RULERS OF HAWAII'S MONARCHY DAYS

KING KAMEHAMEHA I *(ka-MEH-ha-MEH-ha)*
1795 - 1819. Called King Kamehameha the Great, this powerful warrior king united all the Hawaiian Islands under his one sovereign rule.

KING KAMEHAMEHA II ("Iolani Liholiho" — *EE-yo-LAH-ni LEE-ho-LEE-ho)*
1819 - 1824. "Iolani Liholiho" was the son of Kamehameha I. He ascended the Hawaiian throne upon his father's death.

KING KAMEHAMEHA III ("Kauikeaouli" — *KOW-i-KEH-ya-o-OO-li)*
1824 - 1854. A younger son of King Kamehameha I, "Kauikeaouli," ascended the throne upon the death of his brother, "Iolani Liholiho."

KING KAMEHAMEHA IV (Alexander "Liholiho" — *LEE-ho-LEE-ho)*
1854 - 1863. The grandson of Kamehameha I, Alexander "Liholiho" became King Kamehameha IV.

KING KAMEHAMEHA V (Lot — *pronounced as appears)*
1863 - 1872. "Prince Lot," older brother of Kamehameha IV, succeeded to the throne upon his brother's untimely death. He was the last of the Kamehameha dynasty.

KING WILLIAM LUNALILO *(LOO-na-LEE-lo)*
1873 - 1874. A High Chief crowned King by the vote of the people, he was known as the "People's King."

KING DAVID KALAKAUA *(KAH-la-KOW-wa)*
1874 - 1891. Hawaii's last King. Called the "Merry Monarch," he actually placed the Hawaiian crown upon his own head and that of his queen, Kapiolani *(ka-PEE-o-LAH-ni)*.

QUEEN LILIUOKALANI *(li-LEE-u-OH-ka-LAH-ni)*
1891 - 1893. Hawaii's only ruling Queen, she was the sister of King Kalakaua, and the last reigning monarch of Hawaii.

NAME PLACES IN HAWAII

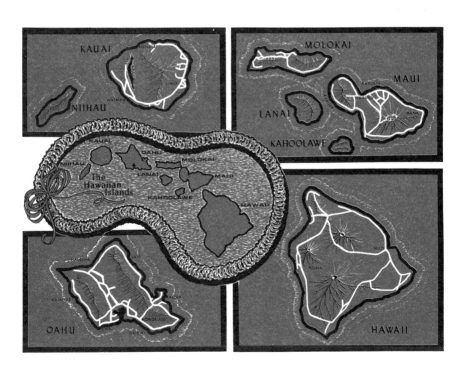

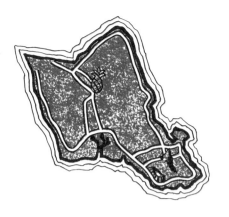

OAHU *(o-WAH-hu)*, called the

"Gathering Place", is the Capital of the Hawaiian chain and third largest of the Islands. Here are name places with which you'll come in contact.

Name places on Oahu:

AALA *(a-AH-la)*
Fragrant, sweet scent.

AHUIMANU *(a-HOO-i-MAH-nu)*
Collection of birds, cluster of birds.

AIEA *(eye-AY-ya)*
Hawaiian Nothocestrum Tree.

AINA HAINA *(EYE-na HEYE-na)*
Land.

ALAKEA *(AH-la-KEH-ya)*
White road; name of a star.

ALA MOANA *(Ah-la mo-WAH-na)*
Sea road.

ALA WAI *(AH-la WEYE)*
Fresh water way.

ALEWA *(a-LEH-va)*
To float cloud-like, buoyant, something suspended.

ANAHULU RIVER *(AH-na-HOO-lu)*
10-day river (perhaps it took 10 days to get there).

AUKAI BEACH *('OW-KEYE)*
Swimming beach.

EHUKAI *(EH-hu-KEYE)*
Name of a wind of Halawa; sea spray; foam.

ELEAO *(e-le-YOW)*
Plant.

EWA *('EH-va)*
Angular or crooked, out of shape. An Oahu direction opposite of Diamond Head, Waikiki and toward Ewa plantation.

HAIKU *(heye-KOO)*
Broken apart.

HALAWA *(ha-LAH-va)*
Curve, as along a beach or in a road, ample trough.

HALEIWA *(ha-le-EE-va)*
House of the frigate bird.

HALEKULANI *(HAH-le-ku-LAH-ni)*
House befitting Royalty.

HALONA *(ha-LOH-na)*
Place to spy from.

HANAUMA *(ha-NOW-ma)*
Curved bay.

HAUULA *(how-'OO-la)*
Red hibiscus hau tree.

HAWAII KAI *(ha-WEYE-'i KEYE)*
Hawaii near the sea.

HEEIA *(he-'EH-ya)*
Slide.

HONOLULU *(HOH-no-LOO-lu)*
Fair haven, sheltered bay, calm harbor, protected harbor.

HONOULIULI *(HOH-no-OO-li-OO-li)*
Bay with dark waters.

HUILUA *(HOO-i-LOO-wa)*
Partner.

HUNAKAI *(hu-na-KEYE)*
Sea spray; sea foam.

IOLANI *(EE-yo-LAH-ni)*
Royal hawk, symbol of royalty because of

its high flight in the heavens.

IWILEI *('i-vi-LAY)*
Collar bone.

KAAAWA *(ka-'a-AH-va)*
The aawa wrasse fish.

KAALA *(ka-AH-la)*
The fragrance.

KAENA *(ka-EH-na)*
The heat.

KAHALA *(ka-HAH-la)*
Amberjack fish; also refers to ripe
gourd and net made of strong cord,
used for sharks.

KAHALUU *(KAH-ha-LOO-'u)*
Diving place.

KAHANA *(ka-HAH-na)*
The work; cutting.

KAHEKILI HIGHWAY *(ka-he-KEE-li)*
The thunder; highway named after a
great chief of the island of Maui known
to be tatooed on one half of his body.

KAHE POINT *(KAH-he)*
To flow.

KAHUKU *(ka-HOO-ku)*
The projection.

KAILUA *(keye-LOO-wa)*
Two currents of the ocean.

KAIMUKI *(keye-mu-KEE)*
Ti-root oven.

KAIOLU *(keye-'OH-lu)*
Pleasant sea.

KAIONA BEACH PARK *(keye-YOH-na)*
Appealing waters.

KAIULANI AVENUE *(ka-EE-yu-LAH-ni)*
Named for the Princess Kaiulani, famed
royal beauty who was heir to the
Hawaiian throne, but never became
queen because of annexation by the
United States.

KAKAAKO *(KAH-ka-'AH-ko)*
Prepare the thatching.

KALAE'O'IO *(ka-LEYE-'OH-'EE-yo)*
The point where the 'o'io fish frequents.

KALAIMOKU *(ka-leye-MOH-ku)*
Named for an early advisor to
Kamehameha the Great.

KALAKAUA AVENUE
(KAH-la-KOW-wa)
Waikiki's main stem, named for the
"Merry Hawaiian Monarch", Kalakaua,
credited with the return of Hawaii's
ancient music and dances.

KALIA *(ka-LEE-ya)*
A nature tree.

KALIHI *(ka-LEE-hi)*
The edge or border.

KAMEHAMEHA HIGHWAY
(ka-MEH-ha-MEH-ha)
A great ruler of the Hawaiian Islands;
well known for uniting the islands under
one rule.

KAMO'OLOA *(ka-MOH-o-LOH-wa)*
The long mo'o (lizard, dragon).

KANEANA CAVE *(KAH-ne-AH-na)*
Kane's cave.

KANEKAPOLEI *(KAH-ne-KAH-po-LAY)*
Name of a Hawaiian Queen, who was
one of the wives of Kamehameha I.

KANEOHE *(KAH-ne-OH-he)*
Bamboo slim man or husband
(refers to a legend).

KAPA *(KAH-pa)*
Tapa cloth made from wauke or
mamaki bark.

KAPAHULU AVENUE *(ka-pa-HOO-lu)*
The worn out sail.

KAPALAMA *(KAH-pa-LAH-ma)*
The lama wood enclosure.

KAPAPA ISLAND *(ka-PAH-pa)*
The flat island.

KAPIOLANI BOULEVARD
(ka-PEE-'o-LAH-ni)
A famous chiefess of Hawaii who defied
Pele; also the name of the queen of
King David Kalakaua.

KAWAILOA *(ka-weye-LOH-wa)*
Long water.

KAWELA *(ka-WEH-la)*
The heat.

KE'AWA HEIAU *(ke-'AH-wa HEH-i-YOW)*
The awa, a place of worship.

KEEHI *(ke-'EH-hi)*
Tread upon.

KEKEPA *(ke-KEH-pa)*
Notched; cut or trimmed obliquely.

KEKEPA ISLAND *(ke-KEH-pa)*
Oblique island.

KE OLU HILLS *(ke OH-lu)*
The pleasant climate.

KEWALO *(ke-WAH-lo)*
The outcry.

KILOHANA *(KEE-lo-HAH-na)*
Best, super, excellent, higher point.

KIPAPA *(ki-PAH-pa)*
Placed prone.

KOKO *(KOH-ko)*
Blood.

KOKOKAHI *(KOH-ko-KAH-hi)*
Place of blood.

KOLEKOLE PASS *(KOH-le-KOH-le)*
Rawness.

KOOLAU *(KOH-'o-LOW)*
Windward.

KUALOA *(KOO-wa-LOH-wa)*
Long back.

KUAMO'O *(KOO-wa-MOH-'o)*
Backbone.

KUAPA POND *(ku-WAH-pa)*
Fish pond made by building a wall
on the reef.

KUHIO AVENUE *(ku-HEE-yo)*
Parallels Kalakaua, a block toward the
mountains; named for Hawaii's Prince,
who served as the first delegate to
congress. Kuhio Beach, a segment of
Waikiki, also is named for the Prince.
Means "path along fresh water".

KUILEI *(ku-i-LAY)*
Wreath braiding.

KUILIMA *(KOO-i-LEE-ma)*
To go arm-in-arm; to hold hands.

KULIOUOU *(KOO-li-OH-OH)*
Bent knee.

KUPIKIPIKIO *(ku-PEE-ki-pi-KEE-yo)*
Agitated, raging, as wind or storm.

LAENANI *(LEYE-NAH-ni)*
Beautiful point.

LAHILAHI *(LAH-hi-LAH-hi)*
Single-flowering, as a hibiscus.

LAIE *(la-EE-e)*
The 'ie vine leaf. Leaf of the 'ie plant.

LANAKILA *(LAH-na-KEE-la)*
Victory.

LANIKAI *(LAH-ni-KEYE)*
Marine heaven.

LANILOA *(LAH-ni-LOH-wa)*
Tall majesty.

LEAHI *(le-AH-hi)*
Hawaiian name for Diamond Head
meaning brow of the ahi fish.

LIKELIKE *(LEE-ke-LEE-ke)*
To equalize; make alike; translate.

LILIUOKALANI *(li-LEE-u-OH-ka-LAH-ni)*
Named for the reigning Monarch,
Queen Liliuokalani of Hawaii.

LUALUALEI *(LOO-wa-LOO-wa-LAY)*
High up (directional).

LUHI PLACE *(LOO-hi)*
Tired place.

LUNALILO *(LOO-na-LEE-lo)*
Flexible wreath. Also name of
Hawaii's sixth king.

MAKAHA *(ma-KAH-ha)*
Fierce.

MAILI *(ma-EE-li)*
Pebbly.

MAKAKILO *(MAH-ka-KEE-lo)*
Over-looking eye.

MAKALAPA *(MAH-ka-LAH-pa)*
Ridge features.

MAKAPUU POINT *(MAH-ka-POO-u)*
Bulging eyes; hill point.

MAKIKI *(ma-KEE-ki)*
Name given to soft porous stone.

MAKILI'I *(MAH-ki-LEE-'i)*
To crack; appear through a crack; come to
light; a sun just appearing in the uplands.

MAKUA *(ma-KOO-wa)*
Parent.

MANANA *(ma-NAH-NAH)*
To stretch out, as arms, fingers, feet;
spread out, protruding. Also the
name of an island.

MANOA *(MAH-no-wa)*
Thick, solid, vast; often referred to
as "The Valley of the Rainbows".

MAUNALANI *(MOW-na-LAH-ni)*
Heavenly mountain.

MAUNALUA *(MOW-na-LOO-wa)*
Two mountains.

MAUNAWILI *(MOW-na-WEE-li)*
Twisting mountain.

MEHA *(MEH-ha)*
Thing.

MILILANI *(MEE-li-LAH-ni)*
To praise, exalt, to give praise, thanks,
to treat as a favorite.

MOANALUA *(mo-AH-na-LOO-wa)*
Two encampments.

MOILI'ILI *(mo-'EE-li-'EE-li)*
Pebble lizard.

MOKAPU *(mo-KAH-pu)*
Restricted ridge; taboo district.

MOKOLI'I *(MOH-ko-LEE-'i)*
Little lizard; name of islet also called
"Chinaman's Hat".

MOKUAU'IA ISLE *(MOH-ku-'OW-'EE-ya)*
Island swimming (in the sea).

MOKULEIA *(MOH-ku-le-EE-ya)*
Amberish.

MOKULUA ISLAND *(MOH-ku-LOO-wa)*
Double islands.

MOKUMANU ISLANDS *(MOH-ku-MAH-nu)*
Bird Island (s).

MOKUPUNI KAO *(mo-ku-POO-ni KOW)*
Goat Island.

NANAKULI *(NAH-na-KOO-li)*
Look deaf, to look at but not respond
when spoken to; to see but pay no
attention to.

NEHOA *(ne-HOH-wa)*
Bold; defiant; daring.

NIU *(NEE-yu)*
Coconut; coco palm.

NUUANU *(NOO-'u-WAH-nu)*
Cool cliffs; cool height.

OLOMANA *('OH-lo-MAH-na)*
Forked hill.

ONEULA BEACH PARK *('OH-ne-'OO-la)*
Reddish sand.

PALAMA *(pa-LAH-ma)*
A sacred and taboo enclosure, especially
for royal women.

PALI *(PAH-li)*
Cliff, precipice.

PALOLO *(pa-LOH-lo)*
White-ish.

PAOAKALANI *(pa-OH-a-ka-LAH-ni)*
Named after an ancient chief of
Kauai Island.

PAUOA *(pow-OH-wa)*
A native fern.

PAU STREET *(POW)*
The end.

PA WA'A *(PAH WAH-'a)*
Canoe enclosure.

PI'IKOI *(PEE-'i-KOY)*
To claim honors not rightfully due,
to seek preference; to aspire to the
best or to more than is one's due.

POKAI *(POH-keye)*
Night of the supreme one.

POPO'IA ISLAND *(po-po-'EE-ya)*
Rounded island.

PUNAHOU *(POO-na-HOH)*
New Spring.

PUNALUU *(POO-na-LOO-'u)*
Coral dived for.

PUPUKEA *(pu-pu-KEH-ya)*
White shell.

ULUNIU *(OO-lu-NEE-yu)*
Coconut grove.

ULUPAU *(OO-lu-POW)*
Everywhere, everything.

WAHIAWA *(WAH-hi-a-WAH)*
Landing place, roaring place.

WAIALAE *(WEYE-a-LEYE)*
Water of the mud hen.

WAIALUA *(WEYE-a-LOO-wa)*
Two streams.

WAIANAE *(WEYE-a-NEYE)*
Mullet water.

WAIAHOLE *(WEYE-ya-HOH-le)*
Waters of the ahole fish.

WAIKANE *(weye-KAH-ne)*
Strong water.

WAIKIKI *(WEYE-ki-KEE)*
Spouting, spurting water.

WAILELE *(weye-LEH-le)*
Waterfall; leaping water.

WAILUPE *(weye-LOO-pe)*
Kite water.

WAIMANLO *weye-ma-NAH-lo)*
Potable water.

WAIMEA *(weye-MEH-ya)*
Reddish water.

WAIOLI *(weye-OH-li)*
Happy water; singing water.

WAIPAHU *(weye-PAH-hu)*
Gushing water.

WAIPIO *(WEYE-PEE-o)*
Arching waters.

NIIHAU *(NEE-'i-HOW)*

Privately owned and largely populated by pure Hawaiians, Niihau is the seventh in size of the main Hawaiian Island group. Known as the "Island of Yesteryear", Niihau means "bound with hau bark".

Name Places on Niihau:

HALALII LAKE *(HAH-la-LEE-'i)*
Named for its owners.

HALULU LAKE *(ha-LOO-lu)*
To roar, thunder, explosion, loud noise, racket.

KAALI CLIFF *(ka-'AH-li)*
Place of ceremonial throwing of spears at high chief. He dodges or catches spears to show his courage and skill.

KAEO *(ka-'EH-yo)*
Full cone.

KAMALINO *(ka-ma-LEE-no)*
Sweet potato.

KIEKIE *(KEE-'e-KEE-'e)*
Lofty.

KII *(KEE-'i)*
Image.

LEHUA *(le-HOO-wa)*
Ohia tree blossom.

NONOPAPA *(NOH-no-PAH-pa)*
Invalid, sick.

PAHAU POINT *(pa-HOW)*
Enclosure or fence of hau trees.

PAKAUA POINT *(PAH-ka-OO-wa)*
Raindrop point.

PUEO POINT *(pu-EH-yo)*
Hawaiian short-eared owl.

PUUKOLE POINT *(POO-'u-KOH-le)*
Upper part of paddle blade joining the handle.

PUUWAI *(POO-'u-WEYE)*
Heart.

KAHOOLAWE *(ka-HOH-'o-LAH-ve)*

In translation, Kahoolawe means "the carrying away." It is an uninhabited island which is called the "Target Island," for it is used by the United States Military Forces for just that — target practice. This small island rates eighth in size in the Hawaiian chain. Presently, there is a controversy over whether the U.S. Military will retain the island or return it to the Hawaiians.

Name Places on Kahoolawe:

KAKA POINT *(KAH-KAH)*
Clean, arched point.

HALONA POINT *(ha-LOH-na)*
Peering place.

KANAPUU BAY *(ka-na-POO-'u)*
Uneven, as a surface or road.

KUKUI POINT *(ku-KOO-wi)*
Candlenut Point.

HAWAII *(ha-WEYE-'i)*

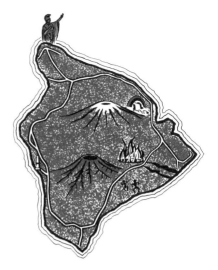

Thought fondly as the Big Island, the "Orchid Isle", and also the "Volcano Isle", Hawaii is the largest of all the other Hawaiian Islands put together. It was named after the believed discoverer and first settler of Hawaii, "Hawaii".

Name Places on Hawaii:

AKAKA FALLS *(a-KAH-ka)*
A split, separating, cleft.

ALAE *('a-LEYE)*
Hawaiian gallinule or mudhen.

ALIKA *(a-LEE-ka)*
Clammy-like.

ALO'I *(a-LOH-'i)*
Mud puddle, pool.

ANAEHO'OMALU
('a-NEYE-HOH-'o-MAH-lu)
Peace offering of anae fish.

HAINA *(ha-EE-na)*
A saying, declaration, statement, question.

HAKALAU *(ha-ka-LOW)*
Many perches.

HALAWA *(ha-LAH-va)*
Ample trough. Curve, as in the road or along a beach. To go from one side to another.

HALEMAUMAU *(HAH-le-MOW-MOW)*
Fern house; fire pit of volcano of Kilauea.

HAMAKUA *(ha-ma-KOO-wa)*
The back of the island; long corner, northeastern side.

HAPUNA *(ha-POO-na)*
Pool, spring.

HAWI *(ha-VEE)*
A time of famine.

HILINA *(hi-LEE-na)*
Struck.

HILO *(HEE-lo)*
First night of the new moon. Name of Polynesian Navigator, Bay & Town.

HOLUALOA *(HOH-LOO-a-LOH-wa)*
Long sliding sled course.

HONAUNAU *(HOH-NOW-NOW)*
Bite, chew.

HONOHINA *(HOH-no-HEE-na)*
Gray bay; gathering place of the goddess, Hina.

HONOKAA *(HOH-no-KAH-'a)*
Cavern, sea cave, deflecting place of the wind. Rolling bay; near seashore with caves.

HONOMU *(HOH-no-MOO)*
Silent bay; gathering of the mu (menehune).

HONU'APO *(HOH-nu-'AH-po)*
Caught turtle; turtle's embrace.

HO'OKENA *(HOH-'o-KEH-na)*
To satisfy thirst; furnish drink.

HUALALAI *(HOO-wa-la-LEYE)*
Obstructing the flow.

HUEHUE *(HOO-'e-HOO-'e)*
To stir up.

HULIHE'E *(HOO-li-HEH-'e)*
Flight, turn.

HUMUULA *(HOO-mu-'OO-la)*
Name of a very hard stone.

KAHALU'U BAY *(KAH-ha-LOO-'u)*
Diving place.

KAILUA *(KEYE-LOO-wa)*
Two currents of the sea; two seas.

KAIMU *(KEYE-MOO)*
Gathering sea.

KAINALIU *(KEYE-na-LEE-yu)*
Bail bilge.

KALAPANA *(KAH-la-PAH-na)*
Shooting field. Announced noted place.

KAMUELA *(ka-mu-WEH-la)*
Samuel; after Samuel Parker, once owner
of Parker Ranch.

KAPAA *(ka-PAH-'a)*
Fast, firm. To hold, as a canoe on its course.

KAPOHO *(ka-POH-ho)*
The hollow.

KA'U *(KAH-'OO)*
The breast; southeast district.

KAUMANA *(KOW-MAH-na)*
The miraculous expression.

KAWAIHAE *(ka-WEYE-HEYE)*
The water of wrath; wild stream.

KEALAKEKUA *(ke-AH-la-ke-KOO-wa)*
Pathway of the gods.

KEANAKAKO'I *(ke-AH-na-ka-KOH-'i)*
The cave of the adze maker.

KEAUHOU *(ke-OW-HOH-u)*
The new era; the new regime.

KEAUKAHA *(ke-OW-KAH-ha)*
The passing current.

KEEAU *(KEH-e-'OW)*
Hindering current.

KE'EI BEACH *(KEH-'AY)*
To peep.

KEIKIWAHA *(KAY-ki-va-ha)*
Talkative child.

KIHOLO *(KEE-HOH-lo)*
A large wooden shark hook.

KOHALA *(ko-HAH-la)*
Pandanus tree; northern district.

KONA *(KOH-na)*
Leeward.

KUKAIAU *(ku-keye-YOW)*
Repeating tide.

KUKUIHAELE *(ku-KOO-i-HEYE-le)*
Traveling light; moving kukui trees.

KULA *(KOO-la)*
Dry upland, pasture, plain, field,
open country.

KULANI *(ku-LAH-ni)*
Like heaven.

KUMUKAHI *(ku-mu-KAH-hi)*
First beginning.

LAUPAHOEHOE *(LOW-pa-HOY-HOY)*
Smooth flat lava; leaf of lava.

LUA MANU *(LOO-wa MAH-nu)*
Bird crater.

MAHUKONA *(MAH-hu-KOH-na)*
Leeward steam or smoke.

MAKAOPUHI *(MAH-ka-o-POO-hi)*
Eel's eye.

MANUKA *(ma-nu-KAH)*
Blundering.

MILOLI'I *(MEE-lo-LEE-'i)*
Little milo tree.

MOKUAWEOWEO
(MOH-ku-wa-WEH-o-WEH-o)
Area of lurid burning; red section.

MO'OKINI *(MOH-'o-KEE-ni)*
Many lizards.

NA'ALEHU *(NAH-'a-LEH-hu)*
Volcanic lava ashes.

(Hawaii, cont'd)

NANILOA *(NAH-ni-LOH-wa)*
Most beautiful.

NAPAU *(na-POW)*
The endings.

NAPO'OPO'O *(na-POH-'o-POH-'o)*
The depressions; an inward depression
of any continuous line (bay).

NINOLE *(ni-NOH-le)*
Bending.

OLAA *(o-LAH-a)*
Of sacredness, dedicated.

ONOMEA *(o-no-MEH-a)*
Something palatable.

'O'OKALA *('OH-'o-KAH-la)*
Sharp digging stick; (sharpened 'o'o).

'OPIHIKAO *('o-PEE-hi-KOW)*
Crowd (gathering) limpets.

PA'AUHAU *(pa-'OW-HOW)*
Tribute yard.

PA'AUILO *(PAH-'a-WEE-lo)*
Maggot infested enclosure.

PAHALA *(pa-HAH-la)*
Cultivation by burning mulch; enclosure
of hala wood.

PAHOA *(pa-HOH-wa)*
Sharp stone; short dagger.

PANA'EWA *(pa-na-'EH-va)*
Crooked shooting.

PAPA'ALOA *(pa-pa-'a-LOH-a)*
Much burned.

PAPA'IKOU *(pa-pa-'i-KOH-u)*
Kou nut tree; kou wood shed.

PAUAHI *(pow-AH-hi)*
Consumed by fire.

PAUKAA *(POW-KAH-'a)*
Completely gone.

PEPE'EKEO *(pe-pe-'e-KEH-yo)*
Food crusted; broken ; bent limb.

POHAKULOA *(po-HAH-ku-LOH-wa)*
Long stone.

POLOLU *(po-lo-LOO)*
Spear.

PUAKO *(POO-a-KOH)*
Sugar cane tassel.

PUNA *(POO-na)*
Coral, lime.

PUNALU'U *(POO-na-LOO-'u)*
Spring dived for.

PU'UANAHULU *(POO-'u-AH-na-HOO-lu)*
Hill roughly formed by erosion.

PU'UEO *(POO-'u-EH-yo)*
Winner hill.

PU'UHULUHULU
(POO-'u-HOO-lu-HOO-lu)
Shaggy hill.

PU'UKOHOLA *(POO-'u-ko-ho-LAH)*
Whale hill.

PU'ULOA *(POO-'u-LOH-wa)*
Long hill.

PU'UWA'AWA'A
(POO-'u-WAH-'a-WAH-'a)
Furrowed hill.

UPOLU *(u-POH-lu)*
Samoan named island; to cover.

UWEKAHUNA *(u-WEH-ka-HOO-na)*
Priestly weeping.

WAHA'ULA *(Wah-ha-'OO-la)*
Red mouth.

WAIAKEA *(WEYE-a-KEH-ya)*
Broad waters.

WAIANUENUE *(WEYE-a-NOO-e-NOO-e)*
Rainbow in water.

WAI'AU *(WEYE-'OW)*
Water to swim in.

WAIKOLOA *(WEYE-ko-LOH-wa)*
Duck water.

WAILOA *(WEYE-LOH-wa)*
Long water.

WAIMEA *(WEYE-MEH-ya)*
Reddish water.

WAILUKU *(WEYE-LOO-ku)*
Waters of destruction.

WAIPIO *(WEYE-PEE-'o)*
Curving water; rainbow-shaped.

WAIMANU *(WEYE-MAH-nu)*
Bird water.

WAOHINU *(WAH-yo-HEE-nu)*
Shiny water; smooth, slick.

LANAI *(LAH-NA-'i)*

The sixth in size in the Island group, Lanai, means "day of contention". It is called the "Pineapple Island", and some-times "The Cinderella Island".

Name places on Lanai:

HALEPALAOA *(HAH-le-pa-LAH-wa)*
Storehouse of whale ivory.

KOELE *(ko-EH-le)*
Rattling.

HALULU *(ha-LOO-lu)*
Legendary man-eating bird.

LANAIHALE *(LAH-NA-'i-HAH-le)*
House of Lanai.

HOOKIO *(HOH-'o-KEE-yo)*
To spread out.

LUAHIWA *(LOO-wa-HEE-va)*
Sacred black pit.

KAHEA *(ka-HEH-ya)*
The sore eyes.

MANELE *(ma-NEH-le)*
Stretcher or litter.

KANEAPUA BAY *(KAH-ne-a-POO-wa)*
Fisherman's bay.

NAHA *(NAH-ha)*
Slit open.

KAIOLOHIA BAY *(KEYE-o-lo-HEE-ya)*
Rough as the sea.

PALAOA POINT *(pa-LAH-wa)*
Whale bay.

KAUMALAPAU *(KOW-MAH-la-POW)*
Soot placed gardens.

PALAWAI *(pa-la-WEYE)*
Pond-scums.

KAUNOLU *(KOW-NOH-lu)*
To give property on a secret wager.

PALOLO POINT *(pa-LOH-lo)*
Whitish clay.

KEOMOKU *(KEH-o-MOH-ku)*
The shortened sand.

POLIHUA *(POH-li-HOO-wa)*
Egg nest.

KIKOA POINT *(ki-KOH-wa)*
Speckled, spotted.

WAIAKEAKUA *(WEYE-a-ke-a-KOO-wa)*
Water of the gods.

MAUI *(MOW-wi)*

Named after the Hawaiian demigod "Maui," who is said to have lassoed the sun so it would travel slowly over the land and favor it with longer days of bright, warming sunshine, Maui is the second largest island in the Hawaiian archipelago. It is often referred to as the "Valley Isle."

Name Places on Maui:

EKE *('EH-ke)*
Bag.

HAIKU *(heye-KOO)*
Broken apart.

HALEKII *(HAH-le-KEE-'i)*
Image house.

HAMAKUAPOKO
(HAH-ma-KOO-wa-POH-ko)
A cultivated field.

HAMOA *(HAH-MOH-wa)*
Fowl trough.

HANA *(HAH-na)*
Work.

HONOKAHUA *(HOH-no-ka-HOO-wa)*
Site's bay.

HONOKOHAU *(HOH-no-ko-HOW)*
Bay drawing dew.

HONOKOWAI *(HOH-no-ko-WEYE)*
Bay drawing water.

HONOLUA *(HOH-no-LOO-wa)*
Two harbors.

HONOMANU *(HOH-no-MAH-nu)*
Bird bay.

HOOLAWA BAY *(HOH-'o-LAH-va)*
To supply.

IAO NEEDLE *('i-YOW)*
Name of Jupiter appearing as the moving star.

IOA *('i-YOH-a)*
Cloud supreme; toward dawn.

KAANAPALI *(ka-'AH-na-PAH-li)*
Rolling precipice.

KAAPAHU BAY *(KAH-'a-PAH-hu)*
To cut off squarely; or crosswise.

KAHAKULOA *(ka-HAH-ku-LOH-wa)*
The tall lord.

KAHANA *(ka-HAH-na)*
Cutting.

KAHULUI *(ka-hu-LOO-wi)*
Gathering together.

KAIWALOA *(KEYE-va-LOH-wa)*
The long fern.

KALAMA *(ka-LAH-ma)*
The torch.

KAMAOLE *(ka-ma-'OH-le)*
Childless.

KAPALUA BEACH *(ka-pa-LOO-wa)*
Two borders.

KAUPO *(KOW-POH)*
Night landing; night season.

KEANAE *(ke-'a-NEYE)*
The mullet.

KEAWAKAPU *(ke-YAH-va-KAH-pu)*
The sacred harbor.

KEOKEA *(ke-yo-KEH-ya)*
The white sand.

KEPANIWAI *(ke-PAH-ni-WEYE)*
The water dam.

KIHEI *(KEE-HAY)*
Shoulder cape.

KIPAHULU FALLS *(KEE-pa-HOO-lu)*
Fetch from exhausted gardens; sojourn
at forest fringe.

KIPAPA *(ki-PAH-pa)*
Pavement.

KOKOMO *(KOH-KOH-MOH)*
Koa tree entrance.

KUAU *(ku-'OW)*
An endemic fern or sea creature.

KULA *(KOO-la)*
Open country.

LAHAINA *(la-HEYE-na)*
Cruel sun.

LAHAINALUNA *(la-HEYE-na-LOO-na)*
Upper Lahaina.

LAUNIUPOKO *(LOW-NEE-yu-POH-ko)*
Short coconut leaf.

LOA LOA HEIAU
(LOH-a LOH-a HEH-i-YOW)
Pitted.

LUALAILUA *(LOO-wa-LEYE-LOO-wa)*
Two-fold tranquility.

MAALAEA BAY *(MAH-'a-LEYE-ya)*
Meaning lost.

MAKAPUU *(ma-ka-POO-'u)*
Bulging eyes.

MAKAWAO *(MAH-ka-WOW)*
Forest beginning; view of wide expanse.

MAKENA *(ma-KEH-na)*
Abundance.

MALA *(MAH-la)*
A cultivated field.

MAUNAOLU *(MOW-na-'OH-lu)*
Cool mountain.

MOKAE COVE *(mo-KEYE)*
A plant.

MOKUPAPA POINT *(mo-ku-PAH-pa)*
Low reef island.

MOLOKINI *(mo-lo-KEE-ni)*
Many ties.

NAHIKU *(NAH-HEE-ku)*
Seven districts.

NAPILI BAY *(na-PEE-li)*
The pili grass.

NUU LANDING *(NOO-'u)*
High place; height.

OLOWALU *('o-lo-WAH-lu)*
Many hills.

PAIA *(pa-'EE-ya)*
Noisy.

PAUWELA *(pow-WEH-la)*
Hot soot.

PIHANA *(pi-HAH-na)*
Fullness.

POHAKU *(po-HAH-ku)*
Rock, stone, mineral, tablet.

POLIPOLI *(POH-li-POH-li)*
Porous rock.

PO'OKANAKA *(POH-'o-ka-NAH-ka)*
Human head.

PUA'A KAA *(pu-WAH-'a KAH-'a)*
Rolling pigs.

PUAA PARK *(pu-WAH-a)*
Scattered; dispersed.

PUKALANI *(POO-ka-LAH-ni)*
Sky opening.

PUU KUKUI *(POO-'u ku-KOO-wi)*
Candlenut hill.

PUUNENE *(POO-'u-NEH-ne)*
Goose hill.

PUU OLAI *(POO-'u 'OH-LEYE)*
Earthquake hill.

ULUPALAKUA
('OO-lu-PAH-la-KOO-wa)
Ripe breadfruit ridge.

WAIANAPANAPA CAVES
(WEYE-'a-NAH-pa-NAH-pa)
Glistening water.

WAIEHU *(WEYE-'EH-hu)*
Water spray.

WAIHEE *(WEYE-HEH-'e)*
Slippery water.

WAIKAPU *(WEYE-KAH-POO)*
Water of the conch.

WAILEA *(WEYE-LEH-ya)*
Water of Lea, goddess of the canoe makers.

WAILUA BAY *(WEYE-LOO-wa)*
Two waters.

WAILUKU *(WEYE-LOO-ku)*
Water of slaughter; breaking waves.

MOLOKAI *(MOH-lo-KAH-'i)*

Meaning "untwisted temple ceremony", Molokai is known as the "Friendly Isle", and is the fifth in size in the Hawaiian Islands.

Name places on Molokai:

HALAWA *(ha-LAH-va)*
Curve as in a road or along a beach, ample trough.

HALEOLONO *(HAH-le-o-LOH-no)*
House of Lono, god of the Makahiki and of peace and prosperity.

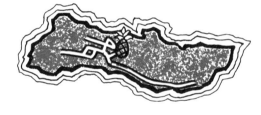

HAUPU BAY *(HAH-'u-pu)*
Memory bay.

HOOLEHUA *(HOH-'o-le-HOO-wa)*
Swift, strong.

ILIO POINT *('i-LEE-yo)*
Dog Point.

KAHIU POINT *(ka-HEE-yu)*
A prayer for victory in battle.

KALAE *(ka-LEYE)*
The clearing.

KALAELOA POINT *(ka-LEYE-LOH-wa)*
Clear distance.

KALAMAULA VALLEY
(ka-LAH-ma-OO-la)
A stone.

KALAUPAPA *(ka-LOW-PAH-pa)*
The flat leaf.

KALAWAO *(ka-la-WOW)*
Designated mountain area.

KALUAOHA *(ka-LOO-wa-OH-ha)*
Double-stranded sacred cord.

KAMAKOU *(KAH-ma-KOH-u)*
The Peucedanum herb.

KAMALO *(ka-ma-LOH)*
The dry place.

KAULAHUKI *(KOW-la-HOO-ki)*
Drawstring or cord to pull on.

KAUNAKAKAI *(KOW-na-ka-KEYE)*
Beach landing.

KAWELA *(ka-VEH-la)*
The heat.

KOLEKOLE *(KOH-le-KOH-le)*
Red earth.

KOLO WHARF *(KOH-lo)*
To creep or crawl, move along as a gentle breeze or shower.

KUALAPUU *(ku-WAH-la-POO-'u)*
Hill overturned; fin protruding.

LAAU POINT *(la-'OW)*
Point of tree, plant, wood or forest.

LEINAOPAPIO *(LAY-na-'o-pa-PEE-'o)*
Spring of the papio fish.

MAHANA *(ma-HAH-na)*
Twins, double; having two branches or forks.

MAKANALUA *(ma-KAH-na-LOO-wa)*
Superior gift; unequalled gift.

MOKU *(MOH-ku)*
To cut, sever, break in two as a rope, to break loose, as a stream after a heavy rain.

MOKUHOONIKI
(MOH-ku-HOH-'o-NEE-ki)
Pinch island.

PALAAU *(pa-la-'OW)*
Wooden fence.

PAPOHAKU BEACH *(PAH-po-HAH-ku)*
Stone wall.

PAUWALU *(POW-WAH-lu)*
By eight, eight-fold, to divide by eight.

PELEKUNU *(PEH-le-KOO-nu)*
Strong smelling.

POPOHAKU *(POH-po-HAH-ku)*
Round bulge or rise.

PUKOO *(pu-KOH-'o)*
Support hill; supporting conch shell.

UALAPUE *('u-WAH-la-POO-'e)*
Hill, as in sweet potatoes.

WAIALUA *(WEYE-ya-LOO-wa)*
Two streams.

WAIHANAU *(WEYE-ha-NOW)*
Birthing water.

WAIKOLU VALLEY *(WEYE-KOH-lu)*
Three waterways.

WAILAU *(WEYE-LOW)*
Many waters.

WAILEIA *(WEYE-LAY-ya)*
Encircling waters.

KAUAI *(kow-WAH-'i)*

Known as both the "Garden Isle" and "Menehune Land", Kauai is the fourth largest island in the Hawaiian group. The name "Kauai" means "to place out to dry", "to dry in the sun", "to light upon". Also, when pronounced with the accent on the second "a" it can mean "the fruitful season" or "time of plenty".

Name places on Kauai:

AAKUKUI VALLEY *(AH-AH-ku-KOO-i)*
Kukui tree root.

AHIHI POINT *(a-HEE-hi)*
Entwined.

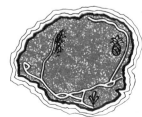

ALAKAI SWAMP (a-la-KAH-i)
To guide.

ALIOMANU (a-LEE-o-MAH-nu)
Bird scream.

ANAHOLA BAY (a-na-HOH-la)
Fish poison cave.

AWAPUHI (a-va-POO-hi)
Ginger.

ELELE ('EH-le-EH-le)
Black.

HAENA (ha-'EH-na)
Heat of the sun, red hot.

HAIKU (HEYE-KOO)
Broken apart.

HALEMANU (HAH-le-MAH-nu)
Bird house.

HALII STREAM (ha-LEE-'i)
A covering for something that is spread out.

HANALEI (ha-na-lay)
Wreath maker, crescent shape bay.

HANAMAULU BAY (ha-na-ma-OO-lu)
Plant cultivation, tired bay.

HANAPEPE (ha-na-PEH-PEH)
To crush, crushed bay.

HAUPU RIDGE (ha-OO-pu)
To recollect; recall, remember.

HOLOHOLOKU (HOH-lo-HOH-lo-KOO)
Run, stand.

HONOPU VALLEY (ho-no-POO)
Gathering together.

HULEIA STREAM (hu-le-EE-ya)
Pumice.

KALAHEO (ka-la-HEH-yo)
Proud day.

KALALAU VALLEY (ka-la-LOW)
The straying, the wanderer.

KALIHIWAI (ka-LEE-hi-WEYE)
Edge of the stream.

KAPA'A (ka-PAH-'a)
The solid, fast, from; land
section and beach park.

KAPA'AU (ka-PAH-'ow)
Land section.

KAPAHI STREAM (ka-PAH-hi)
Standing on edge.

KAPAiA (ka-pa-EE-ya)
The side wall.

KAWAIKINI PEAK (ka-WEYE-KEE-ni)
The multitudinous water. Believed to be
the wettest spot known on earth.

KAWAILOA (ka-WEYE-LOH-wa)
The long water.

KEALIA (ke-a-LEE-a)
The salt encrustation.

KEKAHA (ke-KAH-ha)
The place, land unsuited for growing taro

KILAUEA (ki-la-WEH-ya)
Spewing, much spreading, lookout.

KILOHANA (ki-lo-HAH-na)
Lookout, most beautiful.

KOKEE (ko-KEH-e)
Bend.

KOLOA (ko-LOH-wa)
Wild duck, long sugar cane.

KUKUIOLONO (ku-KOO-i-OH-LOH-no)
Lono's lamp.

LIHUE (li-HOO-'e)
Cold chill; cool breeze.

LUMAHAI (lu-ma-HEYE)
Certain twist of the fingers in making
string figures, perhaps named for a
place on Kauai.

MAKAWELI (MAH-ka-WEH-li)
Fearful eye.

MANA (MAH-NAH)
Arid, satisfied condition.

MANINIHOLO DRY CAVE
(ma-NEE-ni-HOH-lo)
Traveling manini fish.

MOKIHANA *(MOH-ki-HAH-na)*
A fragrant tree.

NAPALI *(na-PAH-li)*
The cliffs.

NAWILIWILI *(NAH-WEE-li-WEE-li)*
The wiliwili tree.

NIUMALU *(NEE-u-MAH-lu)*
Coconut tree shade.

OPAEKAA *(o-PEYE-KAH-'a)*
Rolling shrimp.

POIPU BEACH *(POY-pu)*
Completely overcast, to cover entirely,
as clouds or engulfing waves.

POLIHALE *(POH-le-HAH-le)*
House bosom.

PUHI *(POO-hi)*
Blow.

WAIALEALE MOUNTAIN
(WEYE-'AH-le-'AH-le)
Rippling water, highest mountain
in Kauai, 5,080 ft.

WAIKANALOA *(WEYE-ka-na-LOH-wa)*
Kanaloa's water.

WAIKAPALAE *(WEYE-ka-pa-LEYE)*
Water of the lace fern.

WAILUA *(WEYE-LOO-wa)*
Two waters.

WAIMEA CANYON *(WEYE-MEH-ya)*
Reddish water.

WAINIHA VALLEY *(WEYE-NEE-ha)*
Unfriendly water, wild water.

WAIOLI *(WEYE-'OH-li)*
Singing water.

WAIPAHEE *(WEYE-pa-HEH-'e)*
Slippery water.

WAIPOULI *(WEYE-po-'OO-li)*
Water of darkness.

HAWAII'S STATE FLAG was originated by King Kamehameha I prior to 1816. He ordered it to be designed with eight horizontal red, white and blue stripes representing the eight inhabited islands. Its resemblance to England's "Union Jack" is indicative of Hawaii's early British influence. This flag served as the flag of the Kingdom of Hawaii, the Republic of Hawaii, the Territory of Hawaii and now the State of Hawaii, proudly waving in unison with the United States of America's red, white and blue and its 50 stars, representing its 50 states.

HAWAII STATE CAPITAL CITY

On August 30, 1850, Honolulu was officially declared both a city and the capital of Hawaii. Earlier, capitals were distinguished by virtue of royal residence. Kailua-Kona, where Kamehameha the Great and Kamehameha II resided, remained the capital until Kamehameha III temporarily moved to Lahaina. He moved again in February, 1845, to Honolulu, where the capital has been ever since.

HAWAII'S STATE CAPITOL BUILDING

The architecture of the State Capitol Building, situated near downtown Honolulu, implies the massive grace of a volcano. Prior to its completion in 1969, the Iolani Palace (the only palace in the U.S.) served as the seat of State government.

HAWAII'S STATE SEAL AND MOTTO

The State Seal has its roots in the Kingdom of Hawaii's coat of arms. During Kalakaua's reign, notable changes were made. Modifications continued during its tenure as official seal of the Territory and the Republic. When Hawaii became a state in 1959, the seal consisted of the heraldic shield depicting Kamehameha I on the left and the Goddess of Liberty holding the Hawaiian flag on the right. Below is the Phoenix surrounded by taro leaves, banana foliage and sprays of Maidenhair fern. With the addition of color, this seal also serves as the state's coat of arms. Throughout its history, the seal has carried the motto, "Ua mau ke ea o ka aina i ka pono" ("The life of the land is perpetuated in rightousness"). Kamehameha III spoke these words at a ceremony of thanksgiving at Kawaiahao Church when Rear Admiral Thomas, on behalf of Queen Victoria, returned the government to the Hawaiians after being seized by Lord George Paulet.

HAWAII'S STATE BIRD

The Hawaiian Goose, or Nene *(NEH-ne)*, is the official state bird and the islands' largest land bird. It nearly became extinct before laws were enacted to protect it and restoration projects established to promote growth. The Nene is a shy but determined bird and will fight to the death to defend its goslings.

HAWAII'S STATE SONG

King David Kalakaua composed the state song, "Hawaii Ponoi" (POH-no-ee), which was set to music by the Royal Hawaiian Bandmaster, Captain Henri Berger. It was Hawaii's national anthem in 1876 and acknowledged as state song in 1967.

HAWAII'S STATE FLOWER

The Hibiscus, or "Aloalo" in Hawaiian, is officially designated as the State flower of Hawaii. There are over 5,000 varieties of colors and both single and double blossoms, but the fiery red Hibiscus has come to be the one most widely accepted.

HAWAII'S STATE TREE

The Kukui, also known as the Candlenut Tree (Aleurites moluccana), was proclaimed the state tree in 1959. The ancient Hawaiians prized this tree for its many uses.

Queen Liliuokalani's endearing
musical gift to Hawaii

QUEEN LILIUOKALANI